So You Want To Go To Heaven?
God Tells You How!

Dr. Norman P. Anderson

to Einar Brandingen

May you find my book
a great blessing in your
life. John 14:6.

Dr. Norman P. Anderson

Table Of Contents

ॐ

Introduction

ॐ

Traveling through life, thinking that all is well? Before you know it, it is over! A September 11, 2001, event happens and lives are snuffed out suddenly. If you were one of those people who began the day normally .... then before noon, you are in your eternal destiny, where would you be? "I hope, heaven!" you say. But are you sure you would be in heaven?

God tells us how in the Bible. "But I've tried to read the Bible," you say. "I can't understand it!" I've written this book to help you.

The lack of understanding of the primary message of the Bible is increasing. Parents cannot teach their children God's ways if they themselves do not understand what God has to say about heaven and how to be sure you will get there..

David C. McCasland illustrates this general lack of Bible knowledge when he comments:

"After 30 years as a pastor, a New Jersey minister concluded, "The Bible is the best-selling, least-read, and least-understood book." In his view, "Biblical illiteracy is

rampant." George Gallup, the foremost religion pollster in the U.S. agrees: "We revere the Bible," he says, "but we don't read it." In a recent survey, 64 percent of those questioned said they were too busy to read the Bible. The average household has three Bibles but less than half the people in the U.S. can name the first book of the Old Testament. One survey found that 12 percent of its Christian respondents identified Noah's wife as Joan of Arc!"[1]

This book is a framework for understanding God and the major message of the Bible so you will at least have a knowledge of the purpose and message of the Bible. My prayer is that it will also lead you to make an intelligent commitment of faith to Jesus Christ. When you establish a right relationship with God you can know that you possess eternal life.

There is no more important matter in life than to know that when your Maker calls, you are going to be in your desired destination, heaven.

Dr. Norman P. Anderson

9619 E. Glencove Circle

Prescott Valley, AZ 86314

Endnote

[1] *The Daily Bread,* a daily devotional booklet, published by RBC Ministries, Grand Rapids, Michigan, December 31st, 2001 reading.

Acknowledgments

༄

All of the Scripture references used in this book are taken from the New King James translation. Copyright @ 1979, 1980, 1982 by Thomas Nelson, Inc. Used by permission. All rights reserved.

I dedicate this book to my wonderful life companion, my dear wife, Beverly, who has supported me in ministry and has served by my side through many years. Thank you, Bev, for being God's gracious gift in my life.

I'm very grateful for the editing work of a dear friend, Florence Jacobson. She has helped me immensely to communicate more precisely and with greater clarity.

While I give credit to direct quotes used in this book, there is nothing really original with me. My life has been greatly molded by many professors, pastoral colleagues and friends too numerous to mention. I owe a deep debt of gratitude to all of these wonderful people who have crossed my pathway by the providence of our God. While this book comes from my mind and my heart dedicated to my Savior and Lord, Jesus Christ, it is fashioned by my journey with my many fellow travelers.

CHAPTER ONE

How Can We Know God?

ॐ

If God had not chosen to reveal Himself to mankind, we could not know Him. We would probably have to admit there is something greater holding the universe together, but we need God's Word, the Bible, to understand that <u>something</u> is actually <u>Someone</u>.

God has chosen to reveal Himself in two ways: through the world He has created and through a unique book, the Bible. Chapter two will focus upon what we see revealed about God as the Creator. The rest of this book will give a bird's eye view of the Bible and God's purpose for giving it to us.

The Bible reveals that there is one true God!

Various world religions and various cults propose many other gods. The Bible says there is only one true God! While many other religions claim to believe in the true God, unless the

God we worship is the God revealed in the Bible, the god we worship ends up being a false god of our own creation. We need to allow the Bible to teach us who God is and what He is like.

Before we explore God as our Creator, let's discover some important truths about the Bible.

Here are some facts about the Bible:

- It is one volume made up of 66 different books. God, the author, has used over forty (40) different men to write down His message to us over a period of 1600 years.
- The Bible is different from any other book in that it is inspired by God Himself, revealing Himself and His ways to us.
- God chose a man by the name of Abraham to be the father of the Jewish nation. Then He progressively revealed Himself to the Jewish people so that they may be witnesses to the whole world about Jehovah God.
- The writers that God chose for His revealed word were all Jews except for Luke, who was a Greek.

How can we know the Bible is the word of God?

Let's consider some of the evidences that the Bible is a unique book, the revealed Word of God.

- **The Bible is a unity.** By this we mean that, even though the Bible is written over a period of 1600 years by forty different writers, the Bible is a unit. It is consistent in its message and does not contradict itself. There appear to be some contradictions when one simply does a surface reading rather than a thorough study. However, with study and clear understanding, these apparent contradictions fade away. The unity of the Bible message is consistent from beginning to end.

- **The Bible is historically accurate**. Within its pages there are countless references to events, people and places. Josh McDowell says: "The science of archaeology and secular historical records have repeatedly confirmed the precision of the references in various biblical books. The minute attention to detail observed by biblical writers is unparalleled in any other ancient literature."[1]

- **The Bible is indestructible**. God has preserved His word through careful and accurate copying of manuscripts and through the tedious comparing of various manuscripts that have been preserved for study. We do not have any of the original manuscripts but the accuracy of what we have today is assured. While there are many different translations available in English, any translation done by reputable scholars gives one confidence that this indeed is "God speaking to me." God has also preserved his word in spite of many of its enemies who have set about to eradicate the Bible from existence. The famous atheist Voltaire, who sought to do away with the Bible, died in 1778. It is an irony of history that fifty years after his death, the Geneva Bible Society was using Voltaire's house and printing press to print hundreds of Bibles.

- **The Bible is scientifically accurate**. Although the Bible is not primarily intended to be a scientific textbook, wherever it does speak of scientific matters, it has been proven that it has proven to be accurate. For example, the Bible is not speaking scientifically when it refers to the sun rising and setting, but much in the same way we speak today of the rising and setting of the sun.

- **The Bible is accurate in the fulfillment of prophecies made in the Old Testament**. For example, the Jewish rabbis had identified well over four hundred references to the coming of the Messiah, prophesying details of His birth, His life, His death, His resurrection and His kingly reign.[2] These prophecies about the birth, death and resurrection of the Messiah given hundreds of years before Christ's coming have been fulfilled in precise detail. There are yet many prophecies in the Old and New Testaments concerning things that are yet future. Because of the accuracy of prophecies already fulfilled, we can be confident that these prophecies centering upon the second coming of Jesus Christ and the pending end time judgments will also be fulfilled in precise detail.

- **The Bible is the most accurate book in its insight into the nature of man**. It exposes the sinful nature of every human being and gives us understanding of the inner workings of our souls. Hebrews 4:12 says: *"For the word of God is living and powerful, and sharper than any two-edged sword, piercing even to the division of soul and spirit, and of joints and marrow, and is a discerner of the thoughts and intents of the heart."* The person who seriously reads the Bible to hear God speak to him will soon marvel at the way in which the Bible exposes his real inner self.

What the Bible declares about itself.

- 2 Timothy 3:16 says, *"All Scripture is given by inspiration of God...."*
- 2 Peter 1:20-21 says, *" knowing this first, that no prophecy of Scripture is of any private interpretation, for prophecy never came by the will of man, but holy men of God spoke as they were moved by the Holy Spirit."*

So if you want to know the only true God, and if you want to have a personal relationship with Him, you will discover Him through the Bible. The Psalmist says in Psalm 119:160: *"The entirety of Your word is truth, And every one of Your righteous judgments endures forever."*

My Conclusions

Answers to life's ultimate questions come to us only through God's revelation to us in the Bible. These questions are the tough questions of life. "Who is God?" "What is man's nature and destiny?" "How can I know God personally?" "How can I be in a right relationship with God?" How can I be certain I will go to heaven?" "What is God's plan for saving man from his sin and God's judgment?"

Wise men have grappled with such questions throughout time. But, we cannot find our way to the true God through our own wisdom. We must listen to what God has revealed to us through the Bible.

The apostle Paul shows how inadequate is human wisdom and the philosophies of our sages when he writes in 1 Corinthians 1:18-21:

> *"For the message of the cross is foolishness to those who are perishing, but to us who are being saved it is the power of God. For it is written: "I will destroy the wisdom of the wise, And bring to nothing the understanding of the prudent." Where is the wise? Where is the scribe? Where is the disputer of this age? Has not God made foolish the wisdom of this world? For since, in the wisdom of God, <u>the world through wisdom did not know God, it pleased God through the foolishness of the message preached to save those who believe</u>."*

Through our own intellect and wisdom, we can never discover and know God. Because we cannot discover God and a relationship with God by ourselves, God has graciously chosen to reveal Himself to us in the Bible.

I have studied the Bible since I was very young. I have not blindly accepted its truth but have explored the reasons why the Bible should be believed. I have concluded that the Bible is true and trustworthy to answer life's ultimate questions and it is through the Bible that eternal life is found. The Bible points us to Jesus Christ, God's Son and our Savior. John, the apostle, penned the Gospel of John under the inspiration of the Holy Spirit. He wrote in John 20:30-31: *"And truly Jesus did many other signs in the presence of His disciples, which are not written in this book; but these are written that you may believe that Jesus is the Christ, the Son of God, and that believing you may have life in His name."*

Because the Bible is God's revelation of Himself and His way for mankind to know Him, it is worth your effort to understand it. Your eternal destiny depends upon it.

Endnotes

[1] Josh McDowell, *Five Tough Questions* (Wheaton, Illinois: Tyndale House Publishers, Inc., 1991), p.7.

[2] *Baker Encyclopedia Of The Bible,* Vol. 2, Walter A. Elwell, Editor (Baker Book House, Grand Rapids, Michigan, 1988) p. 1446.

CHAPTER TWO

God Reveals Himself Through Creation

ॐ

Starting at the beginning

The beginning is a very good place to start whether learning the alphabet or learning about the Bible . But it is not really the beginning, for God already existed. Genesis 1:1 says: *"In the beginning God created the heavens and the earth."* So the beginning refers to the beginning of anything that was created or the beginning of anything that had a created existence.

This very first verse of the Bible gives no explanation of God. It simply assumes that He is God and that He has always existed. It is impossible for us to understand how anything, even God, could exist and not have a beginning. However the Bible teaches that God is eternal, that is He has always existed and is above all of His creation.

Psalm 90:1-2 says: *"Lord, You have been our dwelling*

place in all generations. Before the mountains were brought forth, or ever You had formed the earth and the world, even <u>from everlasting to everlasting, You are God.</u>" So before anything existed, God was.

The Creator is One God, in three persons

The only true God is one God who exists in three persons! In our limited mental capacity, this is impossible for us to understand. But the Bible teaches that the one true God is composed of three persons: God the Father, God the Son who is Jesus Christ, and God the Holy Spirit. Because the truth of the Triune God is above our capacity to comprehend, we must simply believe in the Triune God rather than debate how God can possibly exist as one God in three persons. It is abundantly clear as you study the New Testament that the early apostles believed that Jesus Christ and the Holy Spirit were also God and were equal to the Father. Even the commission that Jesus gave to His disciples is based upon the Trinity. Matthew 28:18-20 says, *"And Jesus came and spoke to them, saying, "All authority has been given to Me in heaven and on earth. Go therefore and make disciples of all the nations, baptizing them <u>in the name of the Father and of the Son and of the Holy Spirit</u>, teaching them to observe all things that I have commanded you; and lo, I am with you always, even to the end of the age." Amen."*

The Bible clearly teaches that there is ONE GOD, who exists in three persons. The Scriptural support for the truth of the Triune God is profuse and is best left to further study beyond the scope of this brief birds-eye view of the Bible.

God is the Creator of all things!

He made everything that we can see in our world and in the vast universe around us. John 1:3 says, *"All things were made through Him, and without Him nothing was made that was made."*

John told us that Jesus Christ is the Creator of everything! As the Creator of all things, Jesus could not be merely a created being. He is the Creator of all things and is therefore God, the Creator.

Going back to the beginning, chapter one of Genesis, we find that God created the earth which was formless and void (v. 2). Then on the first day, God created light (vs 3-5); on the second day, He created the air and the sky (vs. 6-8); on the third day, God created the seas and the dry ground and He made all the plants and the trees (vs. 9-13). The fourth day of creation, God created the sun, the moon and the stars (vs.14-19); and on the fifth day of creation, God created all sea life and the birds (vs. 20-23). On the sixth day, God made all the animals, each to reproduce according to its kind, that is dogs reproduce dogs, and lions reproduce lions, etc. (vs 24-25).

The Bible teaches us that God made all of this in preparation to make his last created being, man, to whom He gave the authority to govern the earth. This also was on the sixth day. (vs. 26-27).

God didn't need test-tubes or laboratories

From the following Bible references, we see God creating all things out of nothing. God spoke and everything that He created came into existence as a functional creation. Note that, in Genesis 1, the Bible says time and time again that God said *"Let there be .... and there was......"*

- Psalm 33:6: *"By the word of the Lord the heavens were made, And all the host of them by the breath of His mouth."*

- Psalm 33:8-9: *"Let all the earth fear the Lord; Let all the inhabitants of the world stand in awe of Him. For He spoke, and it was done; He commanded, and it stood fast."*

- Isaiah 44:24: *"Thus says the Lord, your Redeemer, And He who formed you from the womb: "I am the Lord, who makes all things, Who stretches out the heavens all alone, Who spreads abroad the earth by Myself; ......"*

- Hebrews 11:3: *"By faith we understand that the worlds were framed by the word of God, so that the things which are seen were not made of things which are visible."*

- 2 Peter 3:5: *"For this they willfully forget: that by the word of God the heavens were of old, and the earth standing out of water and in the water, ..."*

The Vastness of His creation

Man has invented some powerful telescopes to probe into space. From their discoveries we know that this universe in which we live is just a small part of the vastness that God has created by the word of his power.

Consider our universe. Did you know that if you could bore a hole in the sun and somehow put in 1.2 million earths, you would still have space left over for 4.3 million moons? The sun is 865,000 miles in diameter and 93 million miles away from earth. Pluto, still in our solar system but in the opposite direction, is 2.7 billion miles away. And there may be billions of such solar systems.[1] What are they there for? As best we can determine, they have no other purpose than our enjoyment and perhaps to serve as a challenge to humanity to keep moving ever outward and upward.

Galileo once put it this way, "The sun which has all those planets revolving about it and depending on it for their orderly functions can ripen a bunch of grapes as if it had nothing else in the world to do." God has brought into being a magnificent creation with the sole purpose of providing for His children's needs. Awesome!

The ancient biblical writer, Job, expresses his wonder as he speaks of God as the Creator in Job 26:7-14:

"He stretches out the north over empty space;
He hangs the earth on nothing.
He binds up the water in His thick clouds,
Yet the clouds are not broken under it.
He covers the face of His throne,
And spreads His cloud over it.
He drew a circular horizon on the face of the waters,
At the boundary of light and darkness.
The pillars of heaven tremble,
And are astonished at His rebuke.
He stirs up the sea with His power,
And by His understanding He breaks up the storm.
By His Spirit He adorned the heavens;
His hand pierced the fleeing serpent.
Indeed these are the mere edges of His ways,
And how small a whisper we hear of Him!
But the thunder of His power who can understand?"

It is a good exercise for us humans to ponder the vastness and the awesome creative power of Almighty God as we seek to comprehend His creation. It leads us to humble ourselves before God when we see how small we really are in this vast expanse of creation. If you were to travel through space in a space craft, traveling at the rate of 17,000 miles per hour, it would take you seven months to reach Mars, one of our nearer neighbors. Yet Job says that as we contemplate God's creation, these are *"mere edges of His ways, ..."* just a *"small whisper we hear of Him."*

David Needham writes about God's majesty in creation:

"I was fascinated some time ago by an astronomy journal account about two stars far to the left of the "belt" in the constellation Orion. Though only one star is seen (Procyon is its name), astronomers using elaborate calculations had determined that this star has a tiny twin. By measuring their movements and the distance between the twin stars , they estimated that the smaller star was so compressed, so compacted with power, that a single cubic inch would weigh one hundred tons. Two hundred thousand pounds. Imagine dropping that on your toe!

More recently they have discovered such compression is nothing in comparison to what happens when an entire star explodes. In moments, energy is spewed out equal to that of a billion suns, producing what is called a supernova. At the same time, the star collapses in upon itself to produce a small new star ... a neutron star. Scientists believe these mysterious objects are so compressed that a single cubic centimeter (that's less than a half-inch cube) could weigh at least a hundred billion tons. Maybe a trillion! Some become so dense that the pull of their gravity will not even allow light waves to escape. We call these black holes."[2]

The Psalmist, David, grew up as a shepherd boy and had many nights when he was out under the stars tending the sheep. Such experiences led David to marvel at God's greatness and to wonder why such a great and vast God would pay any attention to him. He expresses this in Psalm 8:3-4: *"When I consider Your heavens, the work of Your fingers, The moon and the stars, which You have ordained, What is man that You are mindful of him, And the son of man that You visit him?"*

Man is God's special creation in that God made man in the image of God. In Genesis 1:26 we read, *"Then God said, "Let Us make man in Our image, according to Our likeness."* Here is a question for your thought: "Who do you think God was speaking about when he said, "Let <u>Us</u> make man in <u>Our</u> image".... Here is the first indication in the Bible of the plurality of persons in the One Godhead. God is speaking about the Father, the Son and the Holy Spirit, the triune God.

What does it mean that God made man in the image of God?

When God made man in His own image, we know that He was not talking about our bodies because God doesn't have a body of flesh and bones like we do. The Bible says, *"God is Spirit"* John 4:24. Rather, God is referring to the part of us which cannot be seen, our soul and our spirit. Man's body was created to be the house of this unseen part, our soul and spirit. Our unseen part has a mind, emotions, and a will created in the image of God. God created us in His image, so that He could have a relationship with us.

The Bible teaches us that there is only One True God who is eternal, existing always, without beginning or ending. He is the Creator of all things that exist and therefore He is Sovereign or King over all things. He alone is worthy of worship and service.

Endnotes

[1] Gleaned from *Dynamic Preaching Magazine,* June, 1991.

[2] David Needham, *Close To His Majesty* (Multnomah Books, Portland, Oregon) p. 20-21.

CHAPTER THREE

The Good News/
Bad News Story

ॐ

In understanding the major message of the Bible we must deal with the good news and the bad news. We've already seen in the last chapter that God made us in His image. That is good news. Now for the bad news Early in the Bible we discover the fall of man into rebellion and sin. Genesis 2 and 3 show us that God created the first human beings, Adam and Eve, and that all people can trace their roots to them.

God placed Adam and Eve in a beautiful and perfect garden setting called Eden. It is thought that Eden was probably somewhere in the Tigris Euphrates River Basin in the region of Mesopotamia, which is part of present day Iraq. Genesis 2:15 tells us that Adam and Eve were placed in Eden and given responsibility for tending the garden. In Genesis 2:16-17 we read God's instructions to man:

"And the Lord God commanded the man, saying,

"Of every tree of the garden you may freely eat; but of the tree of the knowledge of good and evil you shall not eat, for in the day that you eat of it you shall surely die."

Satan Tempts Adam And Eve

Genesis 3 gives us a more complete account of mankind's fall as we read of the serpent's (Satan's) temptation. Who is Satan? In other passages of Scripture like Isaiah 14 and Ezekiel 28, we read that God created spirit beings called angels. Lucifer was an angel of light who rebelled against God and sought to take God's rightful place. So Lucifer was cast out of heaven and took a lot of rebellious created spirit beings with him. They are known in Scripture as Satan and His demons who serve his rebellious purpose.

Satan comes to Eve and tempts her with the tantalizing forbidden fruit and casts doubt upon God's goodness, integrity and trustworthiness. We read of his tempting in Genesis 3:1-5:

"Now the serpent was more cunning than any beast of the field which the Lord God had made. And he said to the woman, "Has God indeed said, 'You shall not eat of every tree of the garden'?" And the woman said to the serpent, "We may eat the fruit of the trees of the garden; but of the fruit of the tree which is in the midst of the garden, God has said, 'You shall not eat it, nor shall you touch it, lest you die.' " Then the

30

serpent said to the woman, "You will not surely die. For God knows that in the day you eat of it your eyes will be opened, and you will be like God, knowing good and evil."

Satan tempts her to commit the same rebellious act that he had committed in time past that resulted in his being cast out of heaven. He tempted her to try to become like God.

Unfortunately, Eve and her husband, Adam, both succumbed to Satan's temptation and ate from the forbidden tree. As a result God placed his curse upon them and upon the physical creation of the earth as well. They were cast out of the garden and ever since, man has had to contend with the results of sin upon this earth. Making a living is a struggle. Weeds for the farmer and pain in child-birth are specifically mentioned as results of sin. Paul, the apostle, says that the whole creation is groaning as it waits for God to redeem this world from its pain and turmoil.

Romans 8:20-22: *"For the creation was subjected to futility, not willingly, but because of Him who subjected it in hope; because the creation itself also will be delivered from the bondage of corruption into the glorious liberty of the children of God. For we know that the whole creation groans and labors with birth pangs together until now."*

What Is Sin?

It is fundamentally a rebellion against God that manifests

itself in self centered and evil ways. It is missing the mark of God's holiness and God's will. The Bible tells us that all of us are sinners because we have inherited a sinful self centered nature from Adam and Eve. We sin because we are born sinners. We are doing what comes naturally to us. Romans 3:23 tells us that *"all have sinned and fall short of the glory of God, ..."*

What Has Sin Done To Us?

The result of our sin is that we are cut off from God and we are dead spiritually. Our relationship with God is completely cut off because our sin separates us from the holy God. Just as Adam and Eve were driven from God's presence, so our sin drives us from God's presence. The apostle Paul says in Romans 6:23: *"For <u>the wages of sin is death</u>, but the gift of God is eternal life in Christ Jesus our Lord."* Sin not only results in physical death but it results in spiritual death. Spiritual death ultimately results in being totally separated from God forever in a place called hell.

The apostle Paul, in Ephesians 2:1-3 describes the condition of each human being before believing in Jesus Christ as Savior.

> *"And you He made alive, who were dead in trespasses and sins, in which you once walked according to the course of this world, according to the prince of the power of the air, the spirit who now works in the*

sons of disobedience, among whom also we all once conducted ourselves in the lusts of our flesh, fulfilling the desires of the flesh and of the mind, and were by nature children of wrath, just as the others."

Spiritually we are dead, completely unable to respond to God. Just as a corpse is unable to do anything at all, so we are unable to do anything that pleases God.

Picture a branch or small limb which is broken off from a tree. When it is broken off from the tree, it may appear to be alive, but what happens in a few days? It becomes totally dead because it no longer can draw life from the tree. We are dead when we are separated from God because He alone is the source of spiritual life.

Mankind Flees Further and Further From God.

As the population of the earth grew, so did the outward expression of man's sin and rebellion against God. By the time we get to Genesis 6, we find that God's patience with man is exhausted. We read in Genesis 6:5-8:

"Then the Lord saw that the wickedness of man was great in the earth, and that every intent of the thoughts of his heart was only evil continually. And the Lord was sorry that He had made man on the earth, and He was grieved in His heart. So the Lord said, "I will destroy man whom I have created from the face of the

earth, both man and beast, creeping things and birds of the air, for I am sorry that I have made them." But Noah found grace in the eyes of the Lord."

One Godly Man, Noah

God commanded Noah to build a huge boat, called an ark, because He was going to destroy all mankind from the face of the earth by sending a world-wide flood. God gave detailed instructions to Noah for building the ark. It was constructed so it could float on the flood of water. It was not meant for traveling on the water. Noah was obedient to God even though all people mocked him as he worked on building the ark over a period of about one hundred and twenty years. So God sent the flood and only Noah, his wife, their three sons and their wives were spared alive. They got onto the ark as God commanded and God caused a pair of each species of animal to get onboard also. Everything and everyone who was not on the ark, died under God's judgment. Only Noah, his wife, their three sons and their wives, and the animals on the ark were spared alive. As men do geological studies of the earth's surface, there are numerous evidences of the flood.

The Bible tells us that a final judgment is coming. All who have not accepted God's way of salvation from His judgment will be judged for their sin and sent away from God to a place called hell. After this bad news chapter, there is good news coming! Just as God provided salvation from the flood for

Noah and his family, God has intervened to provide His way of salvation for all who will trust in Him.

CHAPTER FOUR

God's Plan Required A Savior!

ॐ

Did God Know That Man Would Sin?

God was not caught off guard by the fact that man sinned. God knows all things and nothing is a surprise to Him. Before God ever created anything, he planned a way to redeem man from his sin, to provide a sacrifice for man's sin, so that he might be brought back into a right relationship with Him. 1 Peter 1:18-21 says:

"... knowing that you were not redeemed with corruptible things, like silver or gold, from your aimless conduct received by tradition from your fathers, but with the precious blood of Christ, as of a lamb without blemish and without spot. He indeed was foreordained before the foundation of the world, but was manifest in these last times for you who through Him believe in God, who raised Him from the dead and gave Him glory, so that your

faith and hope are in God."

From before the creation of the world, God planned to send His own Son, Jesus Christ, to die on a cross and to be the sacrifice for our sin. This is revealed throughout the Old Testament and many prophecies tell us of God's unfolding plan.

The First Appearance Of The Gospel

Certainly the full blown gospel about Jesus Christ, as we see it revealed in the New Testament, is not clearly seen. However, the very first promise of the coming Savior is seen in Genesis 3:15:

"And I will put enmity Between you and the woman,
And between your seed and her Seed; He shall bruise
your head, And you shall bruise His heel."

This is the curse that God placed upon Satan when he tempted Eve and caused both Adam and Eve to sin against God. When the Bible speaks here about "you", it is referring to Satan and "the woman" refers specifically to Mary, the mother of Jesus..

The unusual expression "her Seed" infers a virgin birth. The usual expression for the birth of a human being refers to the male or "his seed". God reveals that some special offspring of a woman would crush the Serpent's (Satan's) head and totally defeat Satan. This male child born to a virgin named Mary was Jesus Christ, the Son of God.

The Progressive Revelation Of God's Plan Of Redemption

God's plan of redeeming man from his sin was gradually unfolded in the Old Testament. After God's judgment of the human race through the flood of Noah's time, the population of the earth was gradually being rebuilt but man once again rebelled against God.

God's Judgment Upon The Nations

In Genesis 10 we read of the nations that were being formed through Noah's descendants. In Genesis 11, we find these nations, all speaking one language, uniting to build their tower that reaches to the heavens. They were proud and self sufficient, thinking they could get along without God. The Lord God confused their languages so that they did not understand one another and they were scattered across the earth.

Abraham And The Jewish Nation

In Genesis 12, God selects a specific person, Abram (later named Abraham by God). God calls him to go to Palestine where God chooses to bless him and make a great nation of his descendants, a nation through whom God intended to bless the whole world. Genesis 12:1-3 says:

"Now the Lord had said to Abram: "Get out of your country, From your family

And from your father's house, To a land that I will show you. I will make you a great nation; I will bless you And make your name great; And you shall be a blessing. I will bless those who bless you, And I will curse him who curses you; And in you all the families of the earth shall be blessed."

God blessed Abraham and his barren wife, Sarah, with a miracle son, Isaac, born in their old age when they were past the age of being able to bear children. Isaac and Rebekah had two sons, Jacob and Esau. God chose Jacob by His grace to be the father of twelve sons. Ten of his sons each became the head of one of the tribes of Israel. Each of Joseph's two sons became the head of a tribe also, making twelve tribes. One of the sons of Jacob, Levi, was not given an inheritance of property because he was chosen, with his descendants, to be the priests of Israel.

Slavery In Egypt

During a time of great famine in Israel, Jacob and his family ended up in Egypt and became slaves in Egypt over a period of about four hundred years. But God had not forgotten them and God decreed that they should return to the promised land of Palestine. So He raised up a man named Moses to lead Israel out of Egypt. God brought ten plagues of judgment upon the Egyptians miraculously delivering His people from bondage in Egypt. Israel escaped and eventually possessed the land that had been promised to them. Through Moses, God gave the people His commandments and ordered them to worship Him through a system of sacrifices. God promised to bless them if they would obey Him. You can read this part of the story in the books of Exodus, Leviticus, Numbers, Deuteronomy and Joshua.

A Pattern Of Rebellion By Israel

Over several hundred years, Israel possessed the land but were constantly disobeying God and wandering away from Him. He delivered them frequently from their enemies through specific leaders called judges. As they would repent, God would show His grace and mercy and bring deliverance to them through these judges. There is a book in the Old Testament called Judges that tells about this period of their history.

Israel Seeks A King: The kingdom Of The Jews Established

Soon Israel wanted a king so they could be like other nations. So God relented and granted them a king. King Saul was the first king of Israel but he became a disobedient king and ended his reign in disgrace. God removed the kingdom from Saul and gave it to King David. It is through King David's descendants that God promised to send the Messiah, the Savior He promised in Genesis 3:15. Messiah means

"God's anointed one." Jesus Christ is the fulfillment of numerous Old Testament prophecies that continually pointed to the coming of One who would bear the sins of the world and who would ultimately rule the world in righteousness. "Christ" is the Greek equivalent of the Hebrew word "Messiah".

God's Promises Of A Messiah Savior Fulfilled In Jesus Christ

We have seen that God revealed Himself through creation and He also progressively revealed Himself through His chosen people, Israel. The record of this revelation through Israel is found in the Old Testament of the Bible. In the New Testament, we find the record of the fulfillment of the Old Testament promises of the coming Redeemer, Jesus Christ. God's revealing of Himself through the sending of His Son opens the way completely to sinners that they might be restored to a right relationship to God. Hebrews 1:1-3 says:

"God, who at various times and in various ways spoke in time past to the fathers by the prophets, has in these last days spoken to us by His Son, whom He has appointed heir of all things, through whom also He made the worlds; who being the brightness of His glory and the express image of His person, and upholding all things by the word of His power, when He had by Himself purged our sins, sat down at the right hand of the Majesty on high, ..."

42

Only One Way To Heaven

The Bible is clear that God has provided only one way for man to be reconciled to Himself, that is through His only unique Son, Jesus Christ. This is a stumbling block to many people who prefer to think that there are many ways to come to God. They prefer to believe that all religions have their good points and that we are all going to arrive in heaven some-day. However, such belief is contrary to the revealed truth of God in the Bible.

John 14:6 tells us:

"Jesus said to him,"I am the way, the truth, and the life: no man comes to the Father, except through me."

Acts 4:12 says:

"Nor is there salvation in any other, for there is no other name under heaven given among men by which we must be saved."

Consider the words of Charles Colson, the government official from the Watergate scandal of President Richard Nixon's time, who became a follower of Jesus Christ. He says,

...Jesus' claim does not just assert veracity about Himself; He boldly claims that He is the truth. ...... Jesus does not claim to be just one truth or one real-ity among many, but to be the ultimate reality – the root of what is and what was, the point of origin and framework for all that we can see and know and understand. It is the assertion that in the beginning

was God, that He is responsible for the universe, for our very existence, and that He has created the order and structure in which life exists. Everything we know – all meaning – flows from Him.[1]

Dr. Erwin W. Lutzer speaks about the uniqueness of Jesus when compared to the leaders of other world religions and political leaders. There is no comparison possible, for Jesus stands alone as God, the Son, who has been raised from the dead and is alive forever more. Says Lutzer,

During the Russian revolution of 1918, Lenin said that if Communism were implemented there would be bread for every household, yet he never had the nerve to say, "I am the bread of life; he who comes to Me shall never hunger, and he who believes in Me shall never thirst" (John 6:35).

Hitler made some astounding claims for the role of Germany on this planet, believing that he was beginning a thousand-year Reich (rule). Despite these outlandish claims he never said, "He who believes in the Son has eternal life; but he who does not obey the Son shall not see life, but the wrath of God abides on Him" (John 3:36).

Buddha taught enlightenment; yet he died seeking more light. He never said, "I am the light of the world; he who follows Me shall not walk in darkness, but shall have the light of life" (John 8:12).

Mohammed claimed that he and his tribes were descendants from Abraham through Ishmael, another son of Abraham. But he did not say, "Before Abraham was born, I AM" (John 8:58).

Freud believed that psychotherapy would heal people's emotional and spiritual pains. But he could not say, "Peace I leave with you; My peace I give to you; not as the world gives, do I give to you. Let not your heart be troubled, nor let it be fearful" (John 14:27).

New Age gurus say that all of us will be reincarnated, yet not one of them can say, "I am the resurrection and the life: he that believeth in me, though he were dead, yet shall he live. And whosoever liveth and believeth in me shall never die" (John 11:25).

I urge you to face the question: Who then is Christ? A liar? A lunatic? A legend? Or, Lord? He simply does not allow us the luxury of neutrality.[2]

When you know who Jesus Christ is, then you can understand how He could claim to be the only way to the Heavenly Father or the only way to heaven.

Endnotes

[1] Charles Colson, *The Body, Being Light In Darkness* (Word Publishing, Dallas-London-Vancouver-Melbourne, 1992) p. 152.

[2] Erwin W. Lutzer, *Christ Among Other gods* (Moody Press, Chicago, Illinois, 1994) p. 113, 114.

CHAPTER FIVE

Salvation From Sin Requires The Blood Of Christ!

ॐ

The teaching throughout the Bible, is that redemption from our sins and the restoration of sinful man to a right relationship with God comes only through the shedding of blood.

Why through blood, you ask? Isn't that hideous and gory? No, not when you understand how God views the blood of His Son, Jesus Christ. The Bible clearly teaches that God redeems us from our sins only through the blood of Jesus Christ shed for us on the cross of Calvary. Only in this way do we receive forgiveness of sin and eternal life as a free gift. The blood of Jesus Christ is "the precious blood" (1 Peter 1:18,19). It is repeatedly referred to in the New Testament as "the blood of the covenant" (for example Hebrews 10:29) which God has made with mankind through Jesus Christ, His Son. That blood is to be treated as "holy" or "sacred" because of the value that

God the Father placed upon His Son's sacrifice.

But, we are getting ahead of the story! Let's trace some of the prophetic truths about God's redemptive plan that are clearly seen in the Old Testament.

The Principle Of Atonement

The principle of atonement is plainly laid out in Leviticus 17:11 where we read: *"For the life of the flesh is in the blood, and I have given it to you upon the altar to make atonement for your souls; for it is the blood that makes atonement for the soul."* This is God's established way of covering man's sin. If God has established His chosen way to cover our sin, do you think that He will accept man's proposed way? God is Sovereign which means that His way is the only way. The question which you must ask yourself is "Will I accept God's way or will I insist upon my own man-made way?"

As the Bible proceeds we see this principle unfolded in many ways.

- **God provided a blood sacrifice for Adam and Eve in the garden.**

Genesis 3:7 tells us that, after their deliberate disobedience, Adam and Eve had come to feel their guilt. They covered themselves with their own creation of garments made from fig leaves in their man-made effort to cover over their sin. But God showed them that such a covering was not acceptable to Him! Only God can forgive and cleanse from sin! Only God's way will be effective in removing sin and guilt. So God made them garments from skins that required the shedding of the blood of animals to provide an acceptable covering for their sin. Genesis 3:21.

• **God accepted the blood sacrifice of Abel**.

The first two sons of Adam and Eve were Cain and Abel. Cain was a person who lived his life without trusting God and brought a sacrifice to God from the works of his own hands. Abel believed what God said and brought a sacrifice from his flocks. Abel believed that only through the death of a lamb and the shedding of its blood would he be accepted in God's presence. Genesis 4:4-5 says:

> *"Abel also brought of the firstborn of his flock and of their fat. And the Lord respected Abel and his offering, but He did not respect Cain and his offering. And Cain was very angry, and his countenance fell."*

Conclusively the Bible teaches that atonement is made for an individual by a lamb; in other words a lamb is exchanged for an individual's life. The shedding of blood was required to atone for or to cover sin.

• **God commanded Abraham to sacrifice his only son, Isaac, the miracle child born to Abraham and Sarah in their old age**.

Strange, you say, "God commanding human sacrifice?" However, Abraham does not question God but takes Isaac to

Mount Moriah and places him on the altar, ready to plunge the knife into his son. The angel of the Lord halts his action at the last moment and shows him a ram caught in a thicket. A substitute is provided by God for Isaac! The ram caught in the bushes was killed in his place.. The blood of the ram is given as a substitute for Isaac – again a lamb for an individual.

We are not to conclude from this account of Abraham sacrificing his son, Isaac, that God commands us to sacrifice our children. God made it very clear to his people, Israel, as He gave them the law of Moses that they were forbidden to sacrifice human beings. It was the heathen peoples around them that worshiped false gods in this way. This was a special circumstance designed by God to test Abraham's love and to teach us that God Himself would provide the Lamb as a sacrifice for our sin.

Isaac is a type of Christ here as his father Abraham gives his only son in sacrifice. God, our Heavenly Father has given His only Son as a sacrifice for our sin. The ram is also a type of Christ because the ram became the substitute for Isaac. In the same way Christ, the Lamb, became the substitute sacrifice for us. Hebrews 11:17-19 explains Abraham's action of faith.

"By faith Abraham, when he was tested, offered up Isaac, and he who had received the promises offered up his only begotten son, of whom it was said, "In Isaac your seed shall be called," concluding that God was able to raise him up, even from the dead, from

which he also received him in a figurative sense."

- **Even in the exodus from Egypt, the nation of Israel had to shed blood.**

God called Moses his servant to lead the people of Israel out from under their slavery in Egypt. The Egyptian Pharaoh continually resisted God's command even though many plagues were inflicted by God upon the Egyptians. The last of the ten plagues is the slaying of the first born son in every household. Exodus 11. The plague would also come upon the Israelite homes unless they would be obedient to the command of God and find shelter under the blood of a lamb. In Exodus 12:3 we hear the command of God given through Moses: *"Speak to all the congregation of Israel, saying: 'On the tenth of this month every man shall take for himself a lamb, according to the house of his father, a lamb for a household."*

The animal was to be perfect in every way, speaking to us of the Lord Jesus Christ who was perfect and without sin. Exodus 12:5 says: *"Your lamb shall be without blemish, a male of the first year. You may take it from the sheep or from the goats.'"*

On the fourteenth day of the tenth month, the people of Israel were to slay the lambs. However, that was not enough. They must also apply the blood of the lamb on the doorposts and the lintel of the door in order to protect their families from the death angel who would come through Egypt on that night. Exodus 12:7 instructs them: *"And they shall take some of the blood and put it on the two doorposts and on the lintel of the houses where they eat it."*

The blood of the lamb slain was of no effect unless it was applied. In the same way, the blood of Jesus Christ which was shed for the remission of our sins is of no effect unless it is applied to our lives by God in response to our repentant faith. Note Exodus 12:12-13:

> " *'For I will pass through the land of Egypt on that night, and will strike all the firstborn in the land of Egypt, both man and beast; and against all the gods of Egypt I will execute judgment: I am the Lord. Now the blood shall be a sign for you on the houses where you are. And when I see the blood, I will pass over you; and the plague shall not be on you to destroy you when I strike the land of Egypt."*

Do you see God's way of dealing with sin? A lamb is slain, its blood is shed, as a means of eradicating God's judgment of our sin and our slavery to our sin. Israel's annual celebration of the Passover was to remind them of God's way of redeeming them from slavery . It is still celebrated today by orthodox Jewish families.

- **God provided a system of sacrifice to Israel as a nation to remind them constantly that they were sinners in need of atonement**.

The Day of Atonement ("atonement" means "covering") was a primary day of sacrifice in Israel's worship of God. We read of the Day of Atonement in Leviticus 16. The tabernacle, and later the temple, in which Israel's worship of God was enacted, was divided into two sections, the Holy Place and the Holy of Holies. A heavy curtain (veil) hung between the two sections. An outer court also surrounded the tabernacle which was enclosed by a fence.

A piece of furniture, called the ark of the covenant, was located in the Holy of Holies, the place where God made His presence known. The ark of the covenant was a gold-covered box with a gold-covered lid called the mercy seat. The ark contained the broken tablets of the law which symbolized man's sin against God . Two sculptured golden beings guarded the ark, one on each end of the ark, symbolizing God's holiness and glory.

The high priest had to prepare himself to enter the Holy of Holies in specific ways prescribed by God for his own cleansing from sin. He then sacrificed the lamb by the burnt altar where the lamb was subsequently burned. Then he carried the blood of the lamb into the Holy of Holies where the blood was applied to the mercy seat. When the blood was applied to the mercy seat, God's holiness was satisfied and Israel's sin was covered by the blood. By their obedience in offering the sacrifice in God's prescribed way, the nation was spared from God's judgment upon their sin.

Do you see God's way of redeeming us from our sin? We see a lamb given as a substitute for a nation, pointing to the coming of the Promised One, Jesus Christ, the Lamb of God, who is the Savior of the world. As the writer of Hebrews concludes in Hebrews 9:22: "*And according to the law almost all things are purified with blood, and <u>without shedding of blood there is no remission</u>.*"

Isaiah 53 – A Prophecy 700 Years Before Jesus Was Born

The prophet, Isaiah, writes clearly in chapter 53 of the coming promised Messiah who would be the sacrifice for the sins of mankind. The Messiah who would come would not only be the King of kings who would sit on King David's throne forever, but He would provide atonement for the sins of the world. Note Isaiah's words in Isaiah 53:4-7:

Surely He has borne our griefs

And carried our sorrows;

Yet we esteemed Him stricken,

Smitten by God, and afflicted.

But He was wounded for our transgressions,

He was bruised for our iniquities;

The chastisement for our peace was upon Him,

And by His stripes we are healed.

All we like sheep have gone astray;

We have turned, every one, to his own way;

And the Lord has laid on Him the iniquity of us all.

He was oppressed and He was afflicted,

Yet He opened not His mouth;
He was led as a lamb to the slaughter,
And as a sheep before its shearers is silent,
So He opened not His mouth."

The prophecies of the Old Testament are fulfilled in the coming of Jesus Christ to our world two thousand years ago.

Take up your Bible and read the accounts given by Matthew and Luke of the birth of Jesus to the virgin, Mary. Read about this One born in Bethlehem who was the promised Son to Abraham and to David and by whom all the world would be blessed. Take note of the many times you read the quotations from the Old Testament prophets that were fulfilled precisely by the birth of Jesus. This is known as the Incarnation, God, the Son, taking on human flesh. He became one of us so that He might bring us back to the Father through shedding His blood on the altar of the cross.

God provided His only Son as the Lamb of God who takes away the sin of the world. John, the Baptist, announced to the world who Jesus is as we see it recorded in John 1:29: *"The next day John saw Jesus coming toward him, and said, 'Behold! The Lamb of God who takes away the sin of the world!' "*

John 3:16 is known as the gospel (good news) in a nutshell: *"For God so loved the world that He gave His only begotten*

Son, that whoever believes in Him should not perish but have everlasting life."

He is the Lamb of God for the whole world!

1 Peter 1:18-21 declares *".....knowing that you were not redeemed with corruptible things, like silver or gold, from your aimless conduct received by tradition from your fathers, but with the precious blood of Christ, as of a lamb without blemish and without spot. He indeed was foreordained before the foundation of the world, but was manifest in these last times for you who through Him believe in God, who raised Him from the dead and gave Him glory, so that your faith and hope are in God."*

Jesus is clearly the Passover Lamb who is the fulfillment of all those prophetic Passover lambs that had been slain down through the centuries. Paul, the apostle, refers to Christ as the Passover lamb in 1 Corinthians 5:7 where he says "indeed Christ, our Passover, was sacrificed for us."

In Mark's Gospel we discover that Jesus was put to death on the exact day of Passover. This is more than mere coincidence. The Sovereign God brought it to pass precisely on the day of Passover to demonstrate explicitly that Jesus is the Lamb of God, slain for the sins of the world.

Mark tells us in Mark 14:1-2 that the conspiring chief priests and scribes did not want to put Jesus to death during the feast lest there be an uproar of the people. However, Judas, looking for an opportunity to carry out his treacherous betrayal, found the occasion as Jesus retired to the Garden of Gethsemane to pray. This was after the Passover Supper had been celebrated on the evening of Passover. The Jewish day began at six o'clock in the evening and ended at six o'clock of the next day. By the end of the Passover Day, Jesus had been crucified in the place of all sinners. Could it be more plainly declared by God Himself? Jesus Christ is the Lamb of God who takes away the sin of the world!

The New Testament writer of the book of Hebrews emphasizes that the Old Testament sacrifices were inadequate and that only Christ's sacrificial death takes away our sin. Hebrews 9:11-12 clearly proclaims this truth.

> *"But Christ came as High Priest of the good things to come, with the greater and more perfect tabernacle not made with hands, that is, not of this creation. Not with the blood of goats and calves, but with His own blood He entered the Most Holy Place once for all, having obtained eternal redemption."*

After Jesus Christ died on the cross, shedding his blood for our sins, He entered into the very throne room of God, the Father, there to present His precious blood as the complete sacrifice for our sin. Only this great sacrifice by God, Himself, atones for our sin. For this reason Christ shouted from the cross just before He died, "It is finished!" God's redemptive plan was fulfilled! Every sin you and I have ever committed or ever will commit was atoned for in His perfect sacrifice. Nothing was lacking in payment for our sin! Christ Jesus endured our rightful punishment in hell as the wrath of God against our sin was absorbed in full by Him on the cross.

When Christ died on the cross of Calvary, He was dying in your place and in my place, as our substitute. In Stroudsburg, Pennsylvania, there is a grave of a civil war soldier. The stone bears the date of his birth and death and these words: "Abraham Lincoln's substitute!" President Lincoln recognized that many others were dying that he and many others might live in freedom. Therefore he chose to honor one soldier as a symbol of the many who were dying as substitutes.[1] Have you personalized the message of Romans 5:8? "While Norm was still a sinner, Christ Jesus died for Norm!" If you put your name in those blanks, you will understand that Christ Jesus died as your substitute.

You Must Decide Who Jesus Really Is!

Do you see Him? Jesus Christ is the Lamb of God who takes away the sin of the world. That is who He claimed to be. Hear his claim in Jesus' own words in Mark 10:45: *"For even the Son of Man did not come to be served, but to serve, and to give His life a ransom for many."* As you read the Gospels, Matthew, Mark, Luke and John, you must decide if Jesus Christ is indeed God who became man for the purpose of dying for sinners like you and me?

If you are Jewish, my prayer is that God will open your eyes to see that Jesus Christ is the fulfillment of your hopes and dreams. He is God's Messiah! He is your Savior and your King!

Jesus Christ is more than just a man; He is God, the Son.

In order for someone to die for your sin as a substitute for you, it was necessary for that person to be without sin. Since all human beings are infected with the same disease, namely sin, it took a special act of God Himself to provide the acceptable sacrifice for our sin. Therefore God, the Father, sent His Son, Jesus Christ to be born of a virgin, Mary, by the power of the Holy Spirit. Jesus did not enter the human race from a human father, by the same natural means of conception of all men. Jesus was preserved from the sin of the human race by the Holy Spirit causing Mary to conceive a special child, Jesus, without the role of a human father.

Jesus Christ grew up as a human being and lived with us, living a perfect sinless life. Because of his sinlessness, He became the only acceptable perfect Lamb of God who could bear the sin of the whole world upon Himself when He died on Calvary's cross. Study the following verses:

John 3:16: "For God so loved the world that He gave His only begotten Son, that whoever believes in Him should not perish but have everlasting life."

Romans 5:6-9: *"For when we were still without strength, in due time Christ died for the ungodly. For scarcely for a righteous man will one die; yet perhaps for a good man someone would even dare to die. But God demonstrates His own love toward us, in that while we were still sinners, Christ died for us. Much more then, having now been justified by His blood, we shall be saved from wrath through Him."*

Hebrews 4:14-16: *"Seeing then that we have a great High Priest who has passed through the heavens, Jesus the Son of God, let us hold fast our confession. For we do not have a High Priest who cannot sympathize with our weaknesses, but was in all points tempted as we are, yet without sin. Let us therefore come boldly to the throne of grace, that we may obtain mercy and find grace to help in time of need."*

Hebrews 9:22-28: *"And according to the law almost all things are purified with blood, and without shedding of blood there is no remission. Therefore it was necessary that the copies of the things in the heavens should be purified with these, but the heavenly things themselves with better sacrifices than these. For Christ has not entered the holy places made with hands, which are copies of the true, but into heaven itself, now to appear in the presence of*

God for us; not that He should offer Himself often, as the high priest enters the Most Holy Place every year with blood of another— He then would have had to suffer often since the foundation of the world; but now, once at the end of the ages, He has appeared to put away sin by the sacrifice of Himself. And as it is appointed for men to die once, but after this the judgment, so Christ was offered once to bear the sins of many. To those who eagerly wait for Him He will appear a second time, apart from sin, for salvation."

C. S. Lewis, in my opinion one of the greatest thinkers of all time, believed in Jesus Christ. His comments will clarify for you the magnitude of Jesus claims.

What are we to make of Jesus Christ? This is a question which has, in a sense, a frantically comic side. For the real question is not what are we to make of Christ, but what is He to make of us? The picture of a fly sitting deciding what it is going to make of an elephant has comic elements about it. But perhaps the questioner meant what are we to make of Him in the sense of 'How are we to solve the historical problem set us by the recorded sayings and acts of this Man?' The problem is to reconcile two things . . . On the one side clear, definite moral teaching. On the other claims which, if not true, are those of a megalomaniac, compared with whom Hitler was the most sane and humble of men. There is no half way house and there is no parallel in other religions. . . . The idea of a great moral teacher saying what Christ said is out of the question. In my opinion, the only person who can say that sort of thing is either God or a complete lunatic suffering from that form of delusion which undermines the whole mind of man. If you think you are a poached egg, when you are looking for a piece of toast to suit you, you may be sane, but if you think you are God, there is no chance for you.[2]

Now what is left for you to do? Nothing but to come as a repentant sinner to Jesus Christ and put your trust in what He has done to save you from your sin and all of its penalty. Cease depending upon your goodness and your efforts to make yourself good enough to be accepted by God into heaven. That is man's idea of how to get to heaven, not God's. If you will receive Jesus Christ into your heart and life, he will come into your life and give you new life as a free gift.

Endnotes

[1] Paul Tam, *Encyclopedia of 7,700 Illustrations* (Assurance Publishers, Rockville, Maryland, 1979) p. 1186.

[2] C. S. Lewis, *God In The Dock: Essays On Theology And Ethics* (Wm. B. Eerdmans Publishing Co., Grand Rapids, Michigan, 1978) pp. 156-158.

CHAPTER SIX

Two Possible Destinies

ॐ

Are All People Going To Heaven?

There is a popular belief that God is a God of love and as a God of love He could never send anyone to hell. Many people prefer to believe that all religions have their good points and that all religions are equally valid. After all, we are all headed for the same place! We are just taking different routes to get there. So goes the reasoning.

It is very unpopular to believe that there is only one way to find our way to heaven, that is through Jesus Christ. If you state such a belief, you will likely be viewed today as a narrow minded bigot. You are intolerant to hold such a view. But we have already seen that this is the claim of Jesus Christ Himself. John 14:6 says: *"Jesus said to him, 'I am the way, the truth, and the life. No one comes to the Father except through Me'"*.

In our present world culture, being politically correct is more important than holding on to truth. We have been brain washed into believing that tolerance means accepting all views as being equally valid. True tolerance, on the other hand, means to allow others the freedom to hold their views even though they may be false views. Truth can only be held sincerely when we have the freedom to choose truth or error. This freedom to choose is the right that Adam and Eve were granted by God when He created them.

Now you face the same decision. Will you accept the Bible to be God's revealed word and stand firmly upon what God says? Will you accept what God reveals to us in the Bible as truth? Will you accept the claim of Jesus Christ as God, the Son? Or will you accept the wisdom of men who follow their own reasoning? St. Augustine stated it plainly when he said, *"If you believe what you like in the gospels, and reject what you don't like, it is not the gospel you believe, but yourself."*[1]

The Bible Says There Are Two Roads And Two Destinies

Jesus clearly taught that all people must make a choice about which road they will travel. There are two roads, one leading to eternal life and the other leading to eternal destruction. Read carefully what Jesus taught in Matthew 7:13-14:

"Enter by the narrow gate; for wide is the gate and broad is the way that leads to destruction, and there are many who go in by it. Because narrow is the gate and difficult is the way which leads to life, and there are few who find it."

Jesus tells us that a person must enter the narrow gate in order to be on the difficult way that leads to life. He implies that all are already on the broad way that is leading to destruction. You don't have to do anything to be on the broad road. You must make a decision about entering the narrow gate and ending up on the road that leads to eternal life or heaven. Not to decide means you remain on the broad road. The "narrow gate" is the cross of Calvary upon which Jesus Christ died to bear the sin of the whole world, including your sin and mine. Jesus does not say in this passage of Scripture how one gets on that narrow way to eternal life, but he makes it clear in many other passages of Scripture. You must believe or trust in Jesus Christ as your own personal Savior from sin.

John 3:14-18 says:

And as Moses lifted up the serpent in the wilderness, even so must the Son of Man be lifted up, that <u>whoever believes in Him</u> should not perish but have eternal life. For God so loved the world that He gave His only begotten Son, that <u>whoever believes in Him</u> should not perish but have everlasting life. For God did not send His Son into the world to condemn the world, but that the world through Him might be saved. "<u>He who believes in Him</u> is not condemned; but he who does not believe is condemned already, because he has not believed in the name of the only begotten Son of God."

John 3:36 states:

"*He who believes in the Son has everlasting life; and he who does not believe the Son shall not see life, but the wrath of God abides on him.*"

John 5:24 adds:

"*Most assuredly, I say to you, he who hears My word and believes in Him who sent Me has everlasting life, and shall not come into judgment, but has passed from death into life*".

Paul the apostle underlines the gospel invitation in Romans 10:9-10:

"*..... that if you confess with your mouth the Lord Jesus and believe in your heart that God has raised Him from the dead, you will be saved. For with the heart one believes unto righteousness, and with the mouth confession is made unto salvation.*"

Immortality! What is it?

In every culture around the world and in every individual human being, there is a concept of existence beyond death. This should not seem strange to us for God has made us with an eternal soul. As St. Augustine said long ago, "*Thou hast made us for Thyself, and the heart of man is restless until it finds its rest in Thee.*"[2] When you read of God's creating Adam and Eve in Genesis 1-3, you see that God has made man to have an eternal existence. You soon realize that Adam and

Eve could have had an eternal paradise in the Garden of Eden if they had chosen to obey God. It was their sin and rebellion that disrupted God's eternal plan and brought physical and spiritual death.

Every one of us have an inner sense of the eternal. There is a vacancy that every human being senses until he finds that vacancy filled again by God's presence. Therefore, as you are sensing that lostness, that loneliness, without God, place your faith in Jesus Christ as your Savior and Lord and find that peace that Christ offers to you.

John 14:27:

"Peace I leave with you, My peace I give to you; not
as the world gives do I give to you. Let not your heart
be troubled, neither let it be afraid."

Innately, through God's creative genius, we have a sense of eternal justice. If there was no future time of judgment when justice will be meted out, all of the evil committed in this life would win out. God has placed eternity in the heart of man.

The general definition of immortality is the survival of the soul or spirit of a man after physical death. Every human being will exist somewhere after he dies physically. Hebrews 9:27-28 says:

"And as it is appointed for men to die once, but
after this the judgment, so Christ was offered once
to bear the sins of many. To those who eagerly wait
for Him He will appear a second time, apart from

sin, for salvation."

But is that all there is to immortality? The biblical concept of immortality is much more than the survival of the soul and spirit of man beyond physical death. For the Bible, "immortality" is an immortality of the whole person, body, soul and spirit together. This requires deliverance from the state of death. As an old reliable source puts it:

"It is not a condition simply of future existence, however prolonged, but a state of blessedness, due to redemption and the possession of the 'eternal life' in the soul; it includes resurrection and the perfected life in both soul and body."[3]

Even in the days of the Old Testament, the great sufferer, Job, testified of his confidence in God as Redeemer who would restore him to immortality in his soul and body. Job 19:25-27 says,

"For I know that my Redeemer lives, And He shall stand at last on the earth; And after my skin is destroyed, this I know, That in my flesh I shall see God, Whom I shall see for myself, And my eyes shall behold, and not another. How my heart yearns within me!"

Daniel wrote of that future time of resurrection of the bodies of believers and unbelievers in Daniel 12:2:

"And many of those who sleep in the dust of the earth shall awake, Some to everlasting life, Some to shame

and everlasting contempt."

The great hope for the believer in Jesus Christ is the final resurrection to life beyond this world. It is guaranteed by the resurrection of Jesus Christ from the dead! Because He has been raised from the dead, thus conquering sin and death, believers also shall be raised to their new bodily existence in eternal glory. The apostle Paul writes as he expounds on this great theme of the resurrection from the dead in 1 Corinthians 15:50-57:.

> *"Now this I say, brethren, that flesh and blood cannot inherit the kingdom of God; nor does corruption inherit incorruption. Behold, I tell you a mystery: We shall not all sleep, but we shall all be changed— in a moment, in the twinkling of an eye, at the last trumpet. For the trumpet will sound, and the dead will be raised incorruptible, and we shall be changed. For this corruptible must put on incorruption, and this mortal must put on immortality. So when this corruptible has put on incorruption, and this mortal has put on immortality, then shall be brought to pass the saying that is written: "Death is swallowed up in victory." "O Death, where is your sting? O Hades, where is your victory?" The sting of death is sin, and the strength of sin is the law. But thanks be to God, who gives us the victory through our Lord Jesus Christ."*

Paul, the apostle, teaches the optimistic and blessed hope of the believer that he is immediately in the presence of Jesus Christ upon breathing his last here on this earth. In 2 Corinthians 5:1-8, he describes death as putting off the tent of this flesh and being unclothed but being immediately in the presence of the Lord.

"So we are always confident, knowing that while we are at home in the body we are absent from the Lord. For we walk by faith, not by sight. We are confident, yes, well pleased rather to be absent from the body and to be present with the Lord."

Death for believers, as with the apostle Paul, does not hold fear and dread. Rather it is a more desirable thing than living in this present life. This does not mean that believers are to have a death wish, for life here is to be a fruitful time of service to God by ministering to others. However, death for the believer is the entrance into the presence of the Lord Jesus forever. For this reason death for the believer holds no dread or horror.

Philippians 1:19-23:

"For I know that this will turn out for my deliverance through your prayer and the supply of the Spirit of Jesus Christ, according to my earnest expectation and hope that in nothing I shall be ashamed, but with all boldness, as always, so now also Christ will be magnified in my body, whether by life or by death.

For to me, to live is Christ, and to die is gain. But if I live on in the flesh, this will mean fruit from my labor; yet what I shall choose I cannot tell. For I am hard-pressed between the two, having a desire to depart and be with Christ, which is far better."

The time is coming when Jesus Christ will return a second time to gather His redeemed people to Himself. He will also establish His righteous reign upon this earth. At the time of His coming for believers, they will receive their new bodies, immortal bodies like unto Jesus' own resurrected body. The apostle, Paul, gives this insight in 1 Thessalonians 4:13-18.

"But I do not want you to be ignorant, brethren, concerning those who have fallen asleep, lest you sorrow as others who have no hope. For if we believe that Jesus died and rose again, even so God will bring with Him those who sleep in Jesus. For this we say to you by the word of the Lord, that we who are alive and remain until the coming of the Lord will by no means precede those who are asleep. For the Lord Himself will descend from heaven with a shout, with the voice of an archangel, and with the trumpet of God. And the dead in Christ will rise first. Then we who are alive and remain shall be caught up together with them in the clouds to meet the Lord in the air. And thus we shall always be with the Lord. Therefore comfort one another with these words."

Your Choice!

Do you see who you truly are? You are God's creation, created to be eternally blessed with a personal vital relationship with God Himself. God desires that you might be redeemed from your sin and your impending doom in hell. He is not willing that anyone should perish but that everyone might come to repentance and faith, according to 1 Peter 3:9. You have free choice granted to you by God. It is up to you to respond to His loving provision for you in Jesus Christ. I pray that you will gain Life and Immortality through choosing to trust Christ Jesus as your Savior and Lord.

Endnotes

[1] George Sweeting, *Who Said That?* (Chicago, Moody Press, 1995) p. 61.

[2] George Sweeting, *Who Said That?* (Chicago, Moody Press, 1995) p. 370.

[3] *The International Standard Bible Encyclopedia,* (Wm. B. Eerdmans Publ. Co., Grand Rapids, Michigan, 1939) Vol. III, p. 1459

CHAPTER SEVEN

Hell, What Is It?

ॐ

A Natural Aversion And Resistance To The Teaching Of Hell

Frankly, this is a chapter I would rather not write. Humanly I prefer to write about peace and light and heaven. The thought of anyone having to spend even one second in hell is a thought that breaks my heart..

But this chapter must be written! If I am to be faithful to God, if I am to take seriously the teaching of the Bible, if I am to believe what Jesus Christ Himself said, then I must write clearly and forcefully about hell. And it is just as important that you hear it! Hear it plainly! For if you do not hear about it, and you continue on your own independent way, you will end up there after you leave this life. That will be the most tragic thing you can ever imagine.

Because of this natural repulsion we experience in thinking about hell, some theologians and liberal preachers are seeking to explain away the teaching of hell. Some have remade God to their own preference rather than accepting God as He has revealed Himself in the Bible. Some say that the God of the Old Testament is the God of punishment and wrath while the God of the New Testament is the God of love, mercy and grace. Not so! God has always been and always will be the holy, righteous God who punishes sin and reveals His wrath against sin. God has always been and always will be the God who loves sinners and has provided a way of escape from hell through His Son, Jesus Christ.

Many people fall into the trap of accepting that which appeals to their preferences instead of accepting what the Scriptures reveal.

One very popular preference today is called universalism. Universalism is the view that whereas there is a hell, no one will ever occupy it. After all, universalists say, there are many roads to heaven and everyone will eventually get there. All people will be saved because God is a God of love.

Another appealing preference is annihilationism. It teaches that people who do not accept Christ as their Savior may end up in hell but God will annihilate their souls at some point. So they will suffer for a time but it will not be everlasting in nature. They look at the fires of hell as being consuming fires which end the existence of sinners instead of punishing fires that are eternal in their punishing effects.

H. Richard Niebuhr firmly rebuked the liberal preachers

and theologians who hold such views when he said that they believed in "*a God without wrath [who] brought men without sin into a kingdom without judgment through the ministrations of a Christ without a cross.*"[1]

To leave out the teaching about hell is to sterilize the gospel to fit our human reasoning and our desires. As Larry Dixon has stated it, "*The Gospel presented by many Christians today has no teeth. When the message about Jesus Christ is expressed only in terms of providing a superior joy or peace to that which the world offers, already joyful and peaceful pagans patronize the messenger and ignore the message .... Christians need to faithfully proclaim the complete Gospel. That complete Gospel says, for example, that happiness without holiness is counterfeit Christianity, that self fulfillment and a positive self-image do not bring eternal forgiveness. Such a complete Gospel proclaims that sins must either be pardoned or punished.*"[2]

Jonathan Edwards once said that the reason we find hell so offensive is because of our insensitivity to sin. If we realized the magnitude of our offensive rebellion against God, we would be convinced of God's righteousness in banishing all unforgiven sinners to hell.

The Reality Of Hell

As sure as heaven is a real place, just as certain, hell is a real place! Both places exist in God's created expanse. How do we know? Because the Bible tells us so.

The renowned Baptist preacher, Vance Havner, told of an experience he had as a pastor. *"When I pastored a country church, a farmer didn't like the sermons I preached on hell. He said, "Preach about the meek and lowly Jesus." I said, "That's where I got my information about hell."* [3] The reality of hell is taught plainly by Jesus Christ just as surely as He taught the reality of heaven. Surely He knows whereof He speaks. He is God, the Son, the Creator of all things, including hell itself. Would He come to our world to suffer and die on the cross of Calvary in order to save us if there was no such reality as hell from which to save us? Would He become "sin for us" (2 Corinthians 5:21) to save us from an eternal hell that doesn't really exist? Hear some of the words of Jesus about hell:

- Matthew 10:28: *"And do not fear those who kill the body but cannot kill the soul. But rather <u>fear Him who is able to destroy both soul and body in hell</u>."*
- Mark 9:42-47: *"But whoever causes one of these little ones who believe in Me to stumble, it would be better for him if a millstone were hung around his neck, and he were thrown into the sea. If your hand causes you to sin, cut it off. It is better for you to enter into life maimed, rather than having two hands, <u>to go to hell, into the fire that shall never be quenched— where 'Their worm does not die And the fire is not quenched</u>.' And if your foot causes you to sin, cut it off. It is better for you to enter*

life lame, rather than having two feet, <u>to be cast into</u>
<u>hell, into the fire that shall never be quenched— where</u>
<u>'Their worm does not die And the fire is not quenched.'</u>
And if your eye causes you to sin, pluck it out. It is better
for you to enter the kingdom of God with one eye, rather
than having two eyes, <u>to be cast into hell fire</u>— "

Now take your Bible and find Luke 16:19-31. Read it and
heed the warning of Jesus as he tells of the fate of the rich man
who did not know God and had not found salvation in Jesus
Christ. Verse 23 is clear about the reality of this place of
suffering called hell. *"And <u>being in torments in Hades [hell],</u>*
he lifted up his eyes and saw Abraham afar off, and Lazarus in
his bosom." The expression "Abraham's bosom" is to be
understood as being at the side of Abraham in the presence of
God. John MacArthur notes in his study Bible:

"Abraham's bosom. This same expression (found
only here in Scripture) was used in the Talmud as a
figure for heaven. The idea was that Lazarus was
given a place of high honor, reclining next to
Abraham at the heavenly banquet." [4]

The Necessity Of Hell

The holiness of God necessitates hell. For God to be true
to His own righteous, perfectly holy nature, he must remain
free from any taint of that holiness. To tolerate sin of any
kind would permanently contaminate God and make eternal

righteousness impossible. We long for the coming day when we shall be delivered to an existence in the presence of the holy God where all evil is forever banished and where its re-entrance is an impossibility. Then Jesus Christ will reign in righteousness forever.

Justice necessitates hell. Man's heart has always cried out for justice. A judgment day is coming in which the mills of justice will grind very, very fine and all will be made right! Those who have inflicted great evil upon the world and upon others will receive their just due. When we contemplate the awful evil works of devilish people such as Hitler, Stalin or Osama Bin Laden (you fill in the name of some other tyrant or despicable criminal), hell becomes a necessity. They must get their just due!

Are you ready for this? Sin itself necessitates hell. It is easy to see the justice of a Hitler or a serial killer being sent off to hell by God. Polls show that most people know someone or know of someone that they believe should be in hell. However, they do not believe that they themselves deserve to go to hell. This simply shows our insensitivity to the ugly nature of our sin. Any sin is a horrible, hideous reproach to the holiness of God. The Bible declares, *"all have sinned and fall short of the glory of God ...."* Romans 3:23. It is for this reason that we all are declared to be "the children of wrath" (Ephesians 2:3) who rightly deserve to spend our eternity in hell. Praise God, He has given His Son to rescue us from such a fate.

We do not like to hear about this subject of hell. It is much more pleasant to avoid the subject and to prefer to hear our pastors speak on some more soothing topic. But preaching about hell is necessary in our modern world. Today you will hear more references to "hell" on television and in movies than you will in the churches. If you attend church, when was the last time you can recall a pastor preaching a sermon on hell or warning about God's judgment coming? Even evangelical churches have tended to shy away from preaching and teaching this unpalatable subject because of a desire to appeal to worldly people with sensibility and polish. We do not want to turn off cultured people by "hell fire and brimstone" preaching.

Certainly pastors should not resort to speculative and dramatic preaching that goes beyond what the Bible teaches on the subject of hell. On the other hand, pastors must be faithful in warning of the judgment that is coming and hell that lies beyond the grave for unbelievers. Our silence rocks people to sleep, content to believe that they are in little danger. Larry Dixon puts it this way:

> *"A recent book on the Old Testament is entitled: Loving God and Disturbing Men: Preaching From The Prophets. That's what we Christians are to do: we are to love God and disturb people! Some believers need to hear the Gospel from the perspective of the love of God; others need to be told of the wrath of God. If the biblical doctrine of hell (in all its*

awesomeness as Jesus taught it) won't disturb the second group, nothing will." [5]

As someone has once said, *"the task of the preacher is to comfort the afflicted and to afflict the comfortable."*

The Nature Of Hell

In the Old Testament, the Hebrew word "sheol," translated as grave at times and other times as hell by the old King James Version of the Bible, refers to the place of the departed dead. It primarily refers to the place where the souls of unbelievers are held as they await the time of the final judgment. We will look at just a few references in the Old Testament.

- Deuteronomy 32:22 clearly speaks of a place where God's judgment fires will burn against the rebellious idolaters. *"For a fire is kindled in My anger, And shall burn to the lowest hell (sheol); It shall consume the earth with her increase, And set on fire the foundations of the mountains."*

- Psalm 9:17: "The wicked shall be turned into hell (sheol), And all the nations that forget God."

- The psalmist seeks for God's judgment upon his enemies, those who had claimed to be his friends. Psalm 55:15 says: "Let death seize them; Let them go down alive into hell (sheol), For wickedness is in their dwellings and among them."

- The Psalmist expresses his gratitude to God for delivering his soul from "sheol" in Psalm 86:13: *"For great is Your mercy toward me, And You have delivered my soul from the depths of Sheol."*

The New Testament reveals much more about this eternal place called hell. One of the Greek words used to describe hell is the word "Gehenna." It appears in Matthew 5:22:

"But I say to you that whoever is angry with his brother without a cause shall be in danger of the judgment. And whoever says to his brother, 'Raca!' shall be in danger of the council. But whoever says, 'You fool!' shall be in danger of hell (Gehenna) fire."

Gehenna originally referred to the Valley of Hinnom outside of Jerusalem. In this valley was the garbage dump where the fires burned incessantly. For the Jews Gehenna became the synonym for the place of torment in the future life. Hell can be considered the cosmic garbage dump made by God for the purpose of disposing of all that is evil and would contaminate his eternal kingdom.

The Greek word, "Hades," translated as "hell" by the original King James Version of the New Testament, refers to the place where the souls of unbelievers are held until the final resurrection, when they will appear before God for final sentencing.

They will then be cast into the final eternal hell which is called the lake of fire or the lake of burning brimstone. We read of the final judgment called the Great White Throne of judgment in Revelation 20:11-15:

"Then I saw a great white throne and Him who sat on it, from whose face the earth and the heaven fled away. And there was found no place for them. And I saw the dead, small and great, standing before God, and books were opened. And another book was opened, which is the Book of Life. And the dead were judged according to their works, by the things which were written in the books. The sea gave up the dead who were in it, and Death and Hades delivered up the dead who were in them. And they were judged, each one according to his works. Then Death and Hades were cast into the lake of fire. This is the second death. And anyone not found written in the Book of Life was cast into the lake of fire."

Here are some of the facts that the Bible discloses about this place called hell. Study them and determine to be sure that you will never suffer such a fate.

- Hell is a place where there is eternal punishment. There will be suffering forever. Jesus speaks of a place where *"their worm dies not and the fire is not quenched."* (Previously quoted in Mark 9:44, 46 and 48.) Note also Jesus' words as he teaches about the judgment of the nations at His second coming. Matthew 25:46. *"And these will go away into everlasting punishment, but the righteous into eternal life."*

82

• Hell is a place of fire and burning. Is there literal fire or is this just symbolic? as some say. I believe there is literal fire, although the fire there does not consume but rather torments forever. If it is symbolic of torment, it nevertheless speaks of a horrible place where such burning torment does not end. Even in Hades, the rich man that Jesus refers to in Luke 16, speaks of "being tormented in this flame." (Verse 24). C. S. Lewis states, *"the prevalent image of fire is significant because it combines the ideas of torment and destruction . Now it is quite certain that all these expressions are intended to suggest something unspeakably horrible, and any interpretation which does not face that fact is, I am afraid, out of court from the beginning."* [6]

• Hell is a place prepared for the devil and his evil angels. Matthew 25:41 says: *"Then He will also say to those on the left hand, 'Depart from Me, you cursed, into the everlasting fire prepared for the devil and his angels:'"* God does not desire that any human being should end up in hell. 2 Peter 3:9 says: *"The Lord is not slack concerning His promise, as some count slackness, but is longsuffering toward us, not willing that any should perish but that all should come to repentance."* However, those who resist Christ's appeal of love and His provision of pardon for sin through the cross will be banished to this final eternal dwelling place prepared for Satan and his rebellious angels.

- Hell is a place where the sinner will continue in his sin forever. When the judgment of God is poured out in the end times, even then men will not repent. Rather they will persist in their anger against God and they will blame God for their suffering. Revelation 16:9 says: *"And men were scorched with great heat, and they blasphemed the name of God who has power over these plagues; and they did not repent and give Him glory."* This is the way it will also be in hell. The inhabitants of hell will be firmly set in their rebellion against God forever.

- Hell is a place of banishment from God forever. 2 Thessalonians 1:6-10 describes this final fate for unbelievers. *".... since it is a righteous thing with God to repay with tribulation those who trouble you, and to give you who are troubled rest with us when the Lord Jesus is revealed from heaven with His mighty angels, in flaming fire taking vengeance on those who do not know God, and on those who do not obey the gospel of our Lord Jesus Christ. These shall be punished with everlasting destruction from the presence of the Lord and from the glory of His power, when He comes, in that Day, to be glorified in His saints and to be admired among all those who believe, because our testimony among you was believed."* Some people have said to me, "Well, if I go to hell, at least all my friends will be there also." This will be of little comfort when you wake up to the fact that there is no companionship in hell. Abandoned to Satan and his cohorts, you are surrounded and invaded completely with evil. You are shut out from all that is good and all that has to do with God. What a horrible destiny!

Do you see why this pursuit of your desired destination, heaven, is so critical? It involves avoiding hell, the assured destination of the one who continues on the broad road. You can correct the direction that you are traveling now. Decide to place your faith and trust in Jesus Christ alone and in what He has done for you on the cross. Accept His death on the cross as the payment for your sin. Trust Him for your pardon from sin and hell! At the conclusion of this book you will find further instruction on how to be certain you have eternal life in heaven.

Endnotes

[1] H. Richard Niebuhr, *The Kingdom Of God In America* (Hamden, Conn: Shoe String Press, 1956) p. 193.

[2] Larry Dixon, *The Other Side Of The Good News* (A Bridge Point Book, Victor Books, Wheaton, Illinois, 1992) p. 22.

[3] George Sweeting, *Who Said That?* (Moody Press, Chicago, Illinois, 1994) p. 231.

[4] John MacArthur, *The MacArthur Study Bible* (Word Publishing, Nashville, London, Vancouver, Melbourne, 1997) p. 1548.

[5] Larry Dixon, IBID, p. 186.

[6] C. S. Lewis, *The Problem of Pain* (New York: Macmillan Publishers, 1962) p. 125.

CHAPTER EIGHT

Heaven, What Is It?

ॐ

Is Heaven Just "Pie In The Sky, In the Sweet By And By"?

Skeptics scoff as Christians speak of heaven! "It is just pie in the sky in the sweet by and by!", they say. "It is just a dream, a crutch for weak people to hold onto!" "Both heaven and hell are simply the imaginations of religious zealots who can't face life as it really is!"

Is heaven a reality? Does it really exist somewhere out there? Just as certainly as God exists, and all that He has created exists, so heaven and hell exist. Just as surely as Christ Jesus came, died on a cross and was raised again from the dead, so heaven and hell are real. They are real locations and real destinations, one to be gained and the other to be avoided at all costs.

Many are the skeptics who, in their hour of death, have experienced misery and agony as they go into eternity without faith in Christ Jesus. Contrast this with the death of the true believer in Jesus Christ. Witness the death experience of the Christian and you will witness peace in the midst of physical suffering, confidence in place of fear.

My father, Warren Anderson, came to know Jesus Christ as his personal Savior one evening in his early manhood. From then on he sought to live a life that pleased His Savior. He studied the Bible through his lifetime and sought always to share the "good news" with his neighbors and friends. At the age of 85 years, he was stricken with a fast growing cancer. He was at peace with God, and the last three days before his death, he was hardly conscious. On March 15, 1990, around six in the evening, my mother and my sister stood by his bed as he was ushered into eternity. He had not opened his eyes for three days, but just before he breathed his last, he opened his eyes wide and his face lit up with a smile of excitement. Then he was gone! Where did he go? It is my conviction that he saw the glories of heaven and the person of the Savior, Jesus Christ, beckoning him to come on home.

A word of warning is in order here. Many write of their near death experiences. Do not be too hasty to believe the accounts of seeing the bright light and knowing it was Jesus. Some who write in this way believe things that are very contrary to the Bible's teachings and therefore cannot be writing about the Jesus Christ of the Bible.

Some are, without a doubt, writing about experiences with

Satan's angels of evil, who can take on the appearance of light in order to deceive. One of the most popular of such accounts is Betty Eadie's best seller book, Embraced By The Light.

Take warning! Her teachings are a mixture of Mormonism, New Age religion, and fantasies that make it abundantly clear that her experiences were those of one "embraced by the darkness"[1]

In 2 Corinthians 12:1-6 Paul, the apostle, writes about a man who had an "out of the body" revelation. Bible scholars agree he was writing about his own experience fourteen years previous. Perhaps this occurred when Paul had been stoned and left for dead as he was assaulted for preaching the gospel. He was "caught up into Paradise," [2] he writes. However, he was not free to write the details, as he says he "heard inexpressible words, which it is not lawful for a man to utter."[3]

The apostle Paul also warned about false teachers who professed themselves to be "apostles" and he concludes those warnings with a statement about Satan himself. 2 Corinthians 11:14 says, *"And no wonder! For Satan himself transforms himself into an angel of light."* Study the Bible to discover the truth that God has revealed and that He wants us to know. Then measure what you hear and what you read by the truth of God. The apostle John warns us in 1 John 4:1: *"Beloved, do not believe every spirit, but test the spirits, whether they are of God; because many false prophets have gone out into the world."*

Where Is Heaven?

Usually this question originates with the skeptics also. For, they reason, if you cannot locate heaven and hell somewhere in the cosmic creation, this then proves that such places do not exist.

There is much in the spiritual realm that is invisible! You cannot put God Himself in a test tube and analyze Him in order to prove that He exists. God is Spirit and therefore is not sighted in telescopes or spotted by a microscope on a slide. Yet God exists! There is plenty of evidence of His existence to those who see with the eyes of faith! As the writer of Hebrews says, *"Now faith is the substance of things hoped for, the evidence of things not seen."*[4] Also the writer of Hebrews makes this comment about faith. *"But without faith it is impossible to please Him, for he who comes to God must believe that He is, and that He is a rewarder of those who diligently seek Him."*[5]

Heaven and hell may exist in a spiritual dimension that is totally unknown to us and cannot be located by our physical senses. Certainly man has only explored a small part of what God has created. Therefore heaven and hell may exist in some place in His created cosmos that is as yet unknown and untracked by human genius. As Richard DeHaan comments:

The fact is that vast reaches in space have not yet been probed by the most powerful telescopes. Besides, it is foolish to deny that something exists just because it cannot be seen with the eyes or detected by our present equipment.

Every scientifically minded person in our atomic age realizes that something may be very real while being completely imperceptible to us.[6]

Heaven, A Real Place

The word "heaven" or "heavens" occurs over 600 times in the Bible. Heaven in its singular or plural form refers to three different concepts. First, it is frequently used to refer to the immediate atmosphere around the earth. Secondly, it is often used to refer to space or the cosmic "heavens." The third usage refers to the destination of believers and the home of God. The apostle Paul, while referring to his "out of body" experience in 2 Corinthians 12 refers to being caught up to the *"third heaven."*[7]

Heaven is referred to in a number of other places in the Bible where the word "heaven" is not used. We have already mentioned one other term, "Paradise," which is synonymous with heaven. It is not the scope of this writing to trace all other references. A couple of examples will suffice.

The Psalmist, David, refers to heaven as God's Presence and God's right hand. Psalm 16:11 says, *"You will show me the path of life; In Your presence is fullness of joy; At Your right hand are pleasures forevermore."* Jesus, Himself, taught his disciples about a place that He was preparing for His followers which He calls "My Father's house". John 14:1-3 says: *"Let not your heart be troubled; you believe in God, believe also in Me. In My Father's house are many mansions; if it were not so, I would have told you. I go to prepare a place for you. And if I go and prepare a place for you, I will come again and receive you to Myself; that where I am, there you may be also."* Jesus does not call this a state of being but 'a place.' Indeed, heaven is a real place!

Heaven, God's Dwelling Place

The Bible teaches us that God is present everywhere. In fact, the Psalmist makes it clear that there is no place to which one may flee where he is out of the presence of God.[8] We must not think of God as confined to heaven for He is everywhere. However, heaven is his dwelling place in the sense of being His throne. Heaven is the center of His rule over His creation. Let's review several Scripture passages that indicate that God is in heaven.

- Joshua 2:11: *"And as soon as we heard these things, our hearts melted; neither did there remain any more courage in anyone because of you, for the Lord your God, He is God in heaven above and on earth beneath."*
- 1 Kings 8:30: *"And may You hear the supplication of Your servant and of Your people Israel, when they pray toward this place. Hear in heaven Your dwelling place; and when You hear, forgive."*

- 2 Chronicles 7:14: " *. . . if My people who are called by My name will humble themselves, and pray and seek My face, and turn from their wicked ways, then <u>I will hear from heaven</u>, and will forgive their sin and heal their land.*"
- Job 22:12: "*Is not God in the height of heaven? And see the highest stars, how lofty they are!*"
- Psalm 103:19: "*The Lord has established <u>His throne in heaven</u>, And His kingdom rules over all.*"
- Daniel 4:37: "*Now I, Nebuchadnezzar, praise and extol and honor <u>the King of heaven</u>, all of whose works are truth, and His ways justice. And those who walk in pride He is able to put down.*"
- Matthew 5:48: "*Therefore you shall be perfect, just as your Father in heaven is perfect.*"
- Matthew 6:9: "In this manner, therefore, pray: <u>Our Father in heaven</u>, Hallowed be Your name."

We conclude that God dwells in heaven and He is the Sovereign God who rules from His throne in heaven. We pray to God in heaven and expect God in heaven to hear our prayers as He has promised us.

After his earthly ministry and His resurrection from the dead, Jesus ascended to heaven where He is exalted at "the Father's right hand".[9] The disciples saw Him ascend and the angels (appearing as men) gave witness of His destination. Acts 1:11 reads:

"And while they looked steadfastly toward heaven as He went up, behold, two men stood by them in white apparel, who also said, "Men of Galilee, why do you stand gazing up into heaven? This same Jesus, who was <u>taken up from you into heaven,</u> will so come in like manner as you saw Him go into heaven."

All true believers await His return as He promised. In John 14:3 He promised to *"come again and receive you to Myself that where I am, there you may be also."*

Paul, the apostle, shares with us the hope of the believers in the church at Thessalonica as he writes in 1 Thessalonians 1:9-10:

"For they themselves declare concerning us what manner of entry we had to you, and how you turned to God from idols to serve the living and true God, and <u>to wait for His Son from heaven,</u> whom He raised from the dead, even Jesus who delivers us from the wrath to come."

Heaven, The Destination Of The Saved

The word "saved" is used often in the New Testament to refer to all those who have trusted Jesus Christ's provision of salvation from sin through His death on the cross, where He shed His blood for us. Another term that Jesus used in his conversation with Nicodemus in John 3 is "born again". There he promised that those who are not "born again" would not see the kingdom of God. John 3:3-5 says:

> *"Jesus answered and said to him, "Most assuredly, I*
> *say to you, unless one is born again, he cannot see*
> *the kingdom of God." Nicodemus said to Him, "How*
> *can a man be born when he is old? Can he enter a*
> *second time into his mother's womb and be born?"*
> *Jesus answered, "Most assuredly, I say to you, unless*
> *one is born of water and the Spirit, he cannot enter*
> *the kingdom of God."*

The moment we accept Jesus Christ by faith and trust His atoning blood for our salvation from sin we possess eternal life. Anyone who accepts Jesus Christ as Savior by faith alone is assured of heaven as their home. However we are not completely delivered from the power and the presence of sin in our lives until we die and go home to be with the Lord in heaven. Paul, the apostle gives us a little glimpse of what happens to the believer as he dies. He writes of this in 2 Corinthians 5:1-8:

> *"For we know that if our earthly house, this tent, is*
> *destroyed, we have a building from God, a house not*
> *made with hands, <u>eternal in the heavens</u>. For in this*
> *we groan, earnestly desiring to be clothed with <u>our</u>*
> *<u>habitation which is from heaven</u>, if indeed, having*
> *been clothed, we shall not be found naked. For we*
> *who are in this tent groan, being burdened, not*
> *because we want to be unclothed, but further clothed,*

that mortality may be swallowed up by life. Now He who has prepared us for this very thing is God, who also has given us the Spirit as a guarantee. So we are always confident, knowing that while we are at home in the body we are absent from the Lord. For we walk by faith, not by sight. We are confident, yes, well pleased rather to be absent from the body and to be present with the Lord."

Heaven is described in the Bible as a heavenly city. Hebrews 11:10 speaks of Abraham's intended destiny which he sought by faith. " . . . *he waited for the city which has foundations, whose builder and maker is God."* Abraham was not satisfied with simply possessing his earthly inheritance. He sought his eternal home.

All the great pilgrims of the faith mentioned by the writer of Hebrews lived as "pilgrims and strangers' here on this earth. They had their spiritual eyes set upon a heavenly homeland.

Hebrews 11:16 says of them: *"But now they desire a better, that is, a heavenly country. Therefore God is not ashamed to be called their God, for He has prepared a city for them."*

This same New Testament writer describes the great heritage of the "church of the firstborn," that is the assembly of those who are born again by their faith in Jesus Christ. Hebrews 12:22-24 says:

"But you have come to Mount Zion and to the city of

the living God, the heavenly Jerusalem, to an innu-
merable company of angels, to the general assembly
and church of the firstborn who are registered in
heaven, to God the Judge of all, to the spirits of just
men made perfect, to Jesus the Mediator of the new
covenant, and to the blood of sprinkling that speaks
better things than that of Abel."

Is your name registered in heaven? Do you have your reservation for your place in heaven? The Bible teaches us that God writes your name in His book of Life in heaven when you trust His Son, Jesus Christ to save you from your sin through His blood shed on Calvary's cross. Luke 10:20 says: *"Nevertheless do not rejoice in this, that the spirits are subject to you, but rather rejoice because your names are written in heaven."* In Revelation 20:15 we have this solemn warning: *"And anyone not found written in the Book of Life was cast into the lake of fire."*

The New Heavens And The New Earth

Much is said in the Bible about the end times and the way in which the Lord will bring the world as we know it to a conclusion. We will not even attempt to get into that subject in any detail. However, we want to see the relationship between the heavenly city, the New Jerusalem, and the final state that is described in Revelation 21 and 22 as "the new heaven and the new earth."

John writes in Revelation 21:1: *"Now I saw a new heaven and a new earth, for the first heaven and the first earth had passed away. Also there was no more sea."* Peter gives us insight into a transformation of the heavens and the earth that will take place at the end of time. He speaks of a refining that will come about when the earth and the heavens are purified by fire. 2 Peter 3:10-13 describes this event.

> *"But the day of the Lord will come as a thief in the night, in which the heavens will pass away with a great noise, and the elements will melt with fervent heat; both the earth and the works that are in it will be burned up. Therefore, since all these things will be dissolved, what manner of persons ought you to be in holy conduct and godliness, looking for and hastening the coming of the day of God, because of which the heavens will be dissolved, being on fire, and the elements will melt with fervent heat? Nevertheless we, according to His promise, look for <u>new heavens and a new earth</u> in which righteousness dwells."*

People of our generation who have witnessed the atomic bomb and its effects have no difficulty believing in "elements melting in fervent heat." But this conflagration of the present heavens and earth will not be man-made. Perhaps Jesus Christ, the Maker of the atoms will split the atoms. This will be the purifying judgment of God that will restore the heavens and the earth to their pristine condition before the fall of man into sin.

John describes the heavenly city, the New Jerusalem as it comes down out of heaven and becomes the capital city of the new heavens and the new earth.[10] This will be the final "heaven" which will last for eternity. All sin and evil will be gone.

There will be no more tears and heartaches. Death will have been totally swallowed up and will not enter into God's eternal realm anymore. Dr. John F. MacArthur describes it:

Eternal heaven will be different from the heaven where God now dwells. . . . in the consummation of all things, God will renovate the heavens and the earth, merging His heaven with a new universe for a perfect dwelling-place that will be our home forever. In other words, heaven, the realm where God dwells, will expand to encompass the entire universe of creation, which will be fashioned into a perfect and glorious domain fit for the glory of heaven.[11]

What Will Heaven Be Like?

Well, it won't be boring, that is for sure. The Psalmist describes it as "joys forevermore."[12] We are not given details but we are told that we will reign with Christ forever. We will have plenty to do that will bring glory to our great and mighty God. We will worship Him and exalt the Lord Jesus Christ forever. This does not mean that we will sit around on a cloud and play a harp forever. That is some human imagination of heaven.

We are given just a little glimpse of heaven. John writes about his vision in the best way he can to describe a wonderful place with a wonderful life. He describes this wonderful city, which is the center of the new heavens and the new earth. The dimensions of it are 1500 miles in each direction, width, length and height. One writer says, "At ground level it (the New Jerusalem) covers more area than India, and if placed in the United States would reach from the tip of Maine to the tip of Florida, and from the shores of the Atlantic Ocean westward to Denver.[13] It is a city of pure gold, a gold that is unlike the gold we know. Heavenly gold is clear as glass. Its walls are built of jasper which are built upon foundations that are adorned with all kinds of precious jewels.

The people of God enter in and out of the city as they serve their God who now dwells in the middle of His redeemed people. There are trees of life along and on either side of the pure river of water of life. These trees yield their fruit and the leaves are for the healing or the health of the nations.[14] Genesis begins with Adam and Eve being cast out of the garden of Eden, out of Paradise. Revelation ends with God's redeemed people being restored to Paradise. Genesis pictures angels guarding the gates to the garden so that they could no longer enter into Paradise. Revelation ends with the angel keeping the gates of the city open so that God's redeemed people will never be barred again from God's presence.

It Will Be Worth It All

A Song writer has expressed it this way: "It will be worth it all when we see Jesus."

Life here is filled with troubles and trials. We get weary along the way, dealing with troubles and with pain.

Someday all of this difficult life will be over and we will be able to enjoy heaven forever and forever. Paul, the apostle, who suffered much to share the gospel with the world, says it well.

Romans 8:18: *"For I consider that the sufferings of this present time are not worthy to be compared with the glory which shall be revealed in us."*

1 Corinthians 2:9 says: *But as it is written:* "Eye has not seen, nor ear heard, Nor have entered into the heart of man The things which God has prepared for those who love Him."

Heaven is a wonderful place God is preparing for His children. You don't want to miss it. You don't have to.

Endnotes

[1] For a thorough analysis of Betty Eadie's teachings as compared with Scripture, read John F. MacArthur, *The Glories Of Heaven* (Crossway Books, Wheaton, Illinois, 1996, chapter one.

[2] "Paradise" is another term used synonymously with "heaven". In the New Testament, the word is used three times only. Luke 23:43 – Jesus promises the

repentant thief that on that day, he would be with Him in Paradise. 2 Corinthians 12:4 – Paul's experience. Revelation 2:7 – the promise that overcomers shall "eat from the tree of life, which is in the midst of the Paradise of God."

[3] 2 Corinthians 12:4

[4] Hebrews 11:1

[5] Hebrews 11:6

[6] Richard W. De Haan, *Our Eternal Home* (Radio Bible Class, Grand Rapids, Michigan, p. 11

[7] 2 Corinthians 12:2

[8] Psalm 139:7-12

[9] John 3:13; Ephesians 2:20, 21

[10] Revelation 21:10-27

[11] John F. MacArthur, IBID, p. 89

[12] Psalm 16:11

[13] Richard De Haan, IBID, p. 15

[14] Revelation 22:1-2

CHAPTER NINE

How To Guarantee Your Arrival In Heaven

༈

Sincerity is not enough

The majority of people in our Western World hope that they will be in heaven when they leave this life. Surveys show that most people believe that many roads lead to heaven and that if a person is simply sincere in his beliefs, surely he will make it to heaven. We have shown that such thinking is contrary the teaching of the Bible. Such thinking leads to many people failing to reach their desired destination when they die.

Think about it! You must not only sincerely believe but you must believe in the truth. If what you believe is not true, then it doesn't make any difference how sincerely you believe. God's truth is that we can be saved from our sins and reach heaven when we die only through His provided Savior, Jesus Christ, and through His sacrificial death on the cross.

Suppose you intended to fly to Washington, D.C., from Chicago. If you get on a plane that is headed for Los Angeles, will you arrive in Washington, D.C.? No, regardless of how sincerely you believe you are on the right plane. In the same way, you will not reach your desired destination of heaven if you are not believing in God's provided way of salvation from your sins – no matter how sincere you are about your beliefs.

Head Knowledge Is Not Enough Either

We have gone through the major message of the Bible. You now know intellectually what the facts are. You know that God has provided a way for your sins to be forgiven and for you to become rightly related to the Father again through Jesus Christ. You know that God will grant you the free gift of eternal life if you will believe in His Son, Jesus Christ.

You can know all the facts about Christ and understand what He has done on the cross of Calvary for your sins, but still not get to heaven.

You Must Repent

Jesus made it very clear that repentance is necessary in order to escape God's judgment upon our sin and in order to escape hell. We must not overlook His clear teaching in Luke 13:1-5:

"There were present at that season some who told

Him about the Galileans whose blood Pilate had mingled with their sacrifices. And Jesus answered and said to them, "Do you suppose that these Galileans were worse sinners than all other Galileans, because they suffered such things? I tell you, no; but <u>unless you repent you will all likewise perish</u>. Or those eighteen on whom the tower in Siloam fell and killed them, do you think that they were worse sinners than all other men who dwelt in Jerusalem? I tell you, no; but <u>unless you repent you will all likewise perish</u>."

Jesus says in Luke 15:7 that there is *"more joy in heaven over <u>one sinner who repents</u> than over ninety-nine just persons who need no repentance."* Peter, while preaching on the day of Pentecost (when the Holy Spirit was poured out upon believers) in Acts 2:38, *"<u>Repent</u>, and let every one of you be baptized in the name of Jesus Christ for the remission of sins; and you shall receive the gift of the Holy Spirit."* Peter also writes in 2 Peter 3:9: *"The Lord is not slack concerning His promise, as some count slackness, but is longsuffering toward us, not willing that any should perish but <u>that all should come to repentance</u>."*

There is a common misunderstanding about the nature of repentance. Most people define repentance as "turning away from one's sin." Certainly this is involved. Repent, however, basically means "to change the mind." It is not a matter of changing your way of life for this would be your own self effort, your own good works. This does not bring salvation as we have already seen.

Repentance is a change of your thinking that is brought about by the Holy Spirit of God using the word of God which is God's truth. Note how Paul, the apostle, describes it as he is instructing Timothy about the work of the servant of God in 2 Timothy 2:24-26.

> *"And a servant of the Lord must not quarrel but be gentle to all, able to teach, patient, in humility correcting those who are in opposition, <u>if God perhaps will grant them repentance, so that they may know the truth, and that they may come to their senses</u> and escape the snare of the devil, having been taken captive by him to do his will."*

Repentance is coming to your spiritual senses as your thinking is changed by the Holy Spirit as He uses the truth of God's word in your life. Let's examine what changes in your thinking when the Holy Spirit brings about repentance in your life.

- You think differently about God. You see God as holy and righteous in all His ways. He is perfect in every way and cannot tolerate any taint of sin.
- You think differently about your own sin. Instead of seeing yourself as good enough to get to heaven on your own merit, you see yourself as a sinner. You see yourself

as deserving of God's judgment and punishment. You begin to see how sinful you are in your selfish ways. As one author has put it,

> *"Too many think lightly of sin, and therefore think lightly of the Saviour. He who has stood before God, convicted and condemned, with the rope about his neck, is the man to weep for joy when he is pardoned, to hate evil which is forgiven him, and to live to the honour of the Redeemer by whose blood he has been cleansed."* [1]

- You think differently about Jesus Christ. You now see Him as God, the Son, who died for you that He might rescue you from God's wrath upon your sin. You see Him as the loving Savior who gave Himself that you might have eternal life.

Martyn Lloyd-Jones describes repentance in this way:

> *"Repentance means that you realize that you are a guilty, vile sinner in the presence of God, that you deserve the wrath and punishment of God, that you are hell-bound. It means that you begin to realize that this thing called sin is in you, that you long to get rid of it, and that you turn your back on it in every shape and form . . . That is repentance."* [2]

You must make a personal response by placing your personal faith in Jesus Christ

Jesus Christ has paid the penalty that you rightfully deserve to pay for your sins. He died in your place as your substitute so that you might be forgiven and so that you will never need to face God as your Judge. Jesus Christ rose from the dead and his resurrection from the dead is proof that God, the Father, accepted His shed blood on the cross as full payment for all of your sins.

As Paul the apostle responded to the jailor at Philippi in Acts 16:31: " ..... *Believe on the Lord Jesus Christ, and thou shalt be saved, and thy house..."* There is no decision that you will ever make in your life that will have greater importance than the decision to repent and receive Jesus Christ as your personal Savior. The moment that you make that decision and invite Jesus Christ to be your Savior and Lord, you will be made a member of the family of His redeemed people. You will be given the status of being a child of God forever. Your sin will be forgiven and you are assured of heaven when your earthly life comes to an end.

Realize that Satan seeks to blind you

Satan seeks to keep you from receiving Jesus Christ as your Savior because he desires to keep you in his grasp. If he can keep you from believing in Jesus Christ, you will die and end up in hell, separated from God forever. He will try to get you to feel that you are good enough so that you do not need a Savior. Are you saying "Well, I know I'm not perfect but I'm not all that bad that God would send me to hell!"? Satan will seek to blind your eyes to the seriousness of your sin and he will endeavor to delude you into thinking that God will let you into heaven because you really are not an awful sinner.

If you do see yourself as a sinner, he will seek to keep you thinking that you can make up for your sins by your good works. As long as he can keep you striving to save yourself or pay for your sins by your own good efforts, you will be forever lost from God. Ephesians 2:8-9 says: *"For by grace you have been saved through faith, and that not of yourselves; it is the gift of God, not of works, lest anyone should boast."*

"Grace" means "God doing for us what we do not deserve". So you must receive God's gift of salvation just simply by faith, by believing in Jesus Christ. This gift of salvation doesn't come to you by working for it but by accepting it as God's free gift.

Salvation and heaven is a free but costly gift

A gift is free to us, even though that gift was paid for by the giver. God's gift of salvation was paid for at tremendous cost by God, the Son, Jesus Christ. The minute you seek to pay for a gift, it is no longer a gift. In the same way, salvation is a gift from God to be accepted without any attempt on your part to pay for it. It is by faith without works that you are saved from your sins!

You may ask, "Are good works not important?"

Yes, they are, because you are saved from your sins by Jesus Christ for the purpose of living a life of good works. Ephesians 2:10 says: *"For we are His workmanship, created in Christ Jesus for good works, which God prepared before-hand that we should walk in them."* Good works do not save you from your sins because all of your works as a sinner are all like filthy rags in God's sight (Isaiah 64:6). When you have been saved by Jesus Christ, He lives in you to produce good works by His Holy Spirit's power. So good works are the result of salvation or the fruit of your salvation. After you have trusted Christ as your personal Savior, you want to live a life of good works out of thankfulness to God, not as a means of trying to make yourself right with God.

Only one way, God's revealed way!

Remember, there is no other way given by God to come to the Father, but through His Son, Jesus Christ. The Bible is clear.

Hear the authoritative words of Jesus Himself as recorded in John 14:6: *"Jesus saith unto him, I am the way, the truth, and the life: no man cometh unto the Father, but by me."* Acts 4:12 says: *"Neither is there salvation in any other: for there is none other name under heaven given among men, whereby we must be saved."*

You must place your faith in Him alone, in His death on the cross of Calvary as your substitute, and in His resurrection from the dead. You must open up your life and receive Him into your life, confessing Him as Savior and Lord. Study these verses from the Bible carefully:

John 1:11-13: *"He came to His own, and His own did not receive Him. But as many as <u>received Him</u>, to them He gave the right to become children of God, to those who <u>believe in His name</u>: who were born, not of blood, nor of the will of the flesh, nor of the will of man, but of God."*

Romans 10:9-13: *".... that if <u>you confess with your mouth the Lord Jesus and believe in your heart that God has raised Him from the dead</u>, you will be saved. For with the heart one believes unto righteousness, and with the mouth confession is made unto salvation. For the Scripture says, "Whoever believes on Him will not be put to shame." For there is no distinction between Jew and Greek, for the same Lord over all is rich to all who call upon Him. For "<u>whoever calls on the name of the Lord</u> shall be saved."*

Revelation 3:20: *"Behold, I stand at the door and knock. If anyone hears My voice and <u>opens the door</u>, I will come in to him and dine with him, and he with Me."*

Just as a visitor would knock on the door of your home, asking for you to invite him into your home, so Christ says that He is knocking on the door of your life asking you to invite Him in. If you will open the door and invite Him into your life He will come in and you will be saved from your sin. Christ Jesus will come into your life and live in your life as your Savior and Master.

So now, it is up to you!

What will you do with Jesus Christ? Will you receive Him into your life? If this is your desire, you need to pray to Him (talk to Him). Confess to Christ Jesus that you are a sinner and ask Him to forgive you and to come and live in you. Accept forgiveness from Christ Jesus and receive His free gift of salvation from your sins.

Here is a suggested prayer. Remember, it is not a prayer that saves you. It is trusting (believing in) Jesus Christ that saves you. Prayer is simply how you tell God what you are doing.

Dear God, I know I'm a sinner. I know my sin deserves to be punished. I believe Christ Jesus died for me and rose again from the grave. I repent from my sins and turn to trust Jesus Christ alone as my Savior. Thank you for forgiving my sin and for giving me the gift of eternal life right now. In Jesus name, I pray. Amen.

Now, firm up your decision by putting it in writing. On the last page of this book, there is a document for you to complete. It will remind you in the future of the day when you settled your belief in Jesus Christ as your personal Savior and Lord. You can look back on this day and know that you are born again by God's Spirit, that your sins are all forgiven, and that God has granted you eternal life as a free gift.

If you trusted Jesus Christ as your Savior today, this is the beginning of a relationship with God that is for all eternity. You are a brand new follower of Jesus Christ and you need to begin growing up as a Christian. Get in touch with a good church, one that teaches and preaches this gospel message about which you have now learned. Contact the pastor and let him know of your new decision to trust Christ as your Savior. Let him and the church help you to grow in your new relationship with Christ Jesus.

If you have any questions, please feel free to contact the author at the address listed in the introduction of this book. May God be glorified in your life!

Endnotes

[1] Arnold Dallimore, *Spurgeon* (Banner of Truth Trust, Carlisle, Pennsylvania, 1985) p. 14.

[2] Martyn Lloyd-Jones, *Sermon On The Mount,* (Eerdmans Publishing Co., Grand Rapids, Michigan, 1972) p. 248

APPENDIX A

My Decision To Believe In And To Follow Jesus Christ

ॐ

On this day, _____, in the year _____, I, _____ _____, placed my faith in Jesus Christ as my Savior and Lord. I have allowed Him to come into my life, to forgive my sin and to give me eternal life as His free gift. In gratitude for what He has done for me, I give myself to Jesus Christ, to be His follower from this day forward. By His grace enabling me, I will seek to glorify Him with my life.

Signed: _____

Printed in the United States
17854LVS00006BA/130-510